What a
Way to Go!

What a Way to Go!

PETER BOWLER &
JONATHON GREEN

CHANCELLOR
 PRESS

First published 1983 by Pan Books Ltd

Published in 1994 by Chancellor Press

This 2002 edition published by Chancellor Press, an imprint of
Bounty Books, a division of Octopus Publishing Group,
2-4 Heron Quays, London E14 4JP

Copyright © Peter Bowler 1983

ISBN 0 7537 0581 8

A CIP catalogue record for this book is available from the British Library

Printed in Finland by WS Bookwell Ltd

To **Astrid,**
who gave me the idea
for this book, its title,
and the material
for some of its more startling pages

Contents

Preface

Death comes to us all, and makes us all equal when it
comes. Few would argue with John Donne on that score.
But, great equaliser though the ultimate fact of death may
be, the manner of its coming is far from equitable.

To many, death comes peacefully, in their sleep. For some,
like Pariseau, who was guillotined by mistake in place of
Parisot, the manner of its coming is horribly unfair. For
others, like the tyrant Phalaris, who was roasted to death
within his own bizarre torture machine, the manner of its
coming is extraordinarily appropriate. The instrument of
death may be a mighty hurricane, an erupting volcano, a
dagger, a loose nail or a dangling scarf. The greatest of
people may be laid low by a creature as ignominious as a fly
or a tortoise. Sometimes death comes with a kind of
beauty, as it did to Oliver of Malmesbury, the
eleventh-century Benedictine monk who made himself a
pair of wings and leapt from the top of the highest tower.
On other occasions the coming of death is richly comical –
the ultimate pie in the face.

This book chronicles some of the more surprising, bizarre,
comical, horrific, fantastic, preposterous, sinister,
grotesque, ludicrous or otherwise extraordinary ways in
which death has come to man or woman. Over five
hundred such deaths are recorded. Most of the victims
were real people, but interesting deaths from the realms of
mythology are also included. How, after all, could one
exclude from such a chronicle the inventively macabre

doings of the infamous Medea? I have, by and large, refrained from including the more depressing deaths, even where they may be of some special interest to readers. For example, it is dispiriting to discover how many poets have committed suicide: Chatterton, John Davidson and Sylvia Plath do not appear in these pages. Nor do Charlotte Mew and Vachel Lindsay, both of whom swallowed disinfectant. On the other hand Hart Crane, who leapt into the sea from the stern of an ocean liner, does; there is a kind of grandeur about the manner of his final exit.

A few of the deaths recorded here are not in themselves especially unusual. Some are included because the victims were people whose eminence lends their deaths a degree of interest, even when the manner of their demise was only a little odd. Others are included because of the striking circumstances leading up to their deaths or the curious fate of their corpses. Thus, a bishop's being shot in the stomach, or a retired soldier's being struck by lightning, is not in itself an event that would ordinarily be worthy of record; but when the bishop is shot while practising highway robbery, or when the retired soldier is struck by lightning for the third consecutive time and his grave is subsequently struck by lightning, the event has been regarded as meriting inclusion in these pages. Similarly, an otherwise commonplace murder or suicide committed for an absurd or grotesque reason may be found here, rubbing shoulders with an otherwise commonplace death in which the corpse has been subjected to some particularly macabre form of dissolution, or where there was a degree of grim irony in the attendant circumstances.

In the main, however, the deaths recorded in this book are more or less bizarre. And what a surprising treasure chest of hitherto unknown comedy, horror and grotesquerie they represent! How many of us knew, for example, which famous composer died from hitting himself with his baton while conducting an orchestra; which king of England was killed by having a red-hot length of iron pushed up his anus; which great dramatist was killed by being hit on the head with a tortoise; which ancient philosopher was ground to death in a stone mortar, or which British general was beaten to death with his own wooden leg?

Most of the cases just mentioned relate to famous people; in fact, it comes as something of a surprise to discover just how many eminent people have died in peculiar ways. But there are also many instances of little-known and indeed anonymous people dying in ways so strange that they have gained, in medical textbooks and biographical encyclopaedias, a kind of immortality that they could not have expected and certainly would not have wanted – for example: the sword swallower who accidentally bit through his sword blade, allowing the point to drop fatally into his stomach; the ladies who died from spontaneous combustion; the coalman who was frightened to death by a ventriloquist; the man who died from exhaustion after eighty-seven consecutive orgasms in a single night; and the usurer who was killed by having molten gold poured down his throat. But I am already beginning to anticipate the contents of the ensuing pages. I must rather leave the reader to make his own special discoveries in this storehouse of strange fatalities.

This is not an academic work of reference, and it does not therefore include detailed footnotes or bibliographical information.

My own earlier material comes from sources such as Dr Smith's *Classical Dictionary*, Brewer's *Dictionary of Phrase and Fable*, Gibbon's *Decline and Fall of the Roman Empire*, Tacitus' *Annals of Ancient Rome*, the anonymous *Augustan History* and Maunder's *Biographical Treasury*. Some of my later material comes from turn-of-the-century texts in medicine and forensic medicine, in particular the fascinating *Anomalies and Curiosities in Medicine* by G. M.

Gould and W. L. Pyle, Glaister's *Medical Jurisprudence and Toxicology*, Haydn's *Dictionary of Dates* and Harvey's *Oxford Companion to English Literature*, storehouses of surprising amounts of information about the byways and back alleys of mortality. In more recent times, a wealth of detail about unnatural deaths has been given in the many books that have been written by or about the great coroners, detectives and forensic pathologists of this century – people such as Spilsbury, Camps, Purchase and Helpern – and in the many popular accounts of famous murders. Much of this last material is in fact available from a variety of sources, the more notable murders being dealt with by many different authors and editors. Finally, one other source has provided some of the most interesting items recorded in this book: the mass of ephemeral, often sensational, reportage of daily events available to us in our newspapers and magazines.

It is a pity that some of the cases recorded in these pages cannot, because of the nature of the source from which the information was obtained, be more fully documented. This applies particularly to the more ephemeral sources just mentioned, but also to some of the more substantial. One frustrating defect already touched upon is the absence in so many cases of the victim's name. In other instances we have the name or at least the surname, but little else. Such deficiencies must remain inevitable in a book of this kind, and I have not excluded particular entries merely on that account.

I end this preface with a quotation from one of the great Elizabethans – Sir Francis Bacon: 'Death hath this also; that it openeth the gate to good fame, and extinguisheth envy.'

No one will envy those whose deaths are recorded in these pages; few will begrudge them their peculiar kind of fame

Murder most foul

Anonymous boy *(impaled on a poker)*

A boy was killed by having a red-hot poker thrust up his anus. He and some other boys had been annoying a tailor who was working in a workshop just underneath the footpath. The tailor had thrust the poker through an iron grating to frighten the boys away, just as one of them was squatting against the other side of the iron bars.

Anonymous gold prospectors *(killed and eaten 1873)*

Twenty novice gold prospectors set out to search for gold in Colorado's San Juan Mountains in the icy winter of 1873. They met up with an expert, one Albert Packer, who promised to lead them to a certain strike. So bad was the weather that half of the twenty gave up the adventure before they had even set out, but the remainder picked up rations from some friendly Indians and followed Packer into the frozen mountains. The weather worsened and the party divided. Six decided to stay put; the other four, plus their guide, forged on. The blizzards intensified and the luckless party, trapped in a lonely hut, ate their last meal and prepared for death – all, that was, but Alfred Packer. As the others slumped over into exhausted sleep, Packer moved quickly from man to man, shooting each in the back of the head. The fourth man tried to struggle, but Packer smashed in his head with a rifle butt. Searching through their packs, Packer extracted several thousand dollars. Then he prepared for his journey home, butchering the

corpses and freezing the meat in a snow drift. At first he
could hardly stomach the awful rations but, as the trip
progressed, Packer found himself a whole-hearted
cannibal. On his return suspicions were at once aroused.
Why had Packer survived when the others had died, where
had he obtained the money he was spending so liberally
and, most disturbingly, how come he was so sleek and
plump after a journey the horrors of which he was at
constant pains to describe? A search party set out and soon
confirmed what had only been awful theory: there were
four skeletons, their wounds still obvious, their flesh
stripped methodically away. At the trial that followed – a
trial that Packer survived only because the Colorado
constitution had no apparatus for conferring the death
penalty – the judge, a lifelong Democrat, underlined his
distaste, exclaiming: 'Packer, you depraved son of a bitch,
there were only four Democrats in Hinsdale County, and
you ate them all!' Packer served sixteen years of a
forty-year term for manslaughter, then died, quite
peacefully, while working on a Colorado ranch in 1907.

Anonymous South African black *(killed 1947)*

A black man was standing at a bus stop in Johannesburg
when two whites approached. Referring to his gloves they
told him he was 'too well dressed'. At which point they
knocked him down and beat him with a large stone. He
died of his injuries.

Anonymous victims
(of the original 'Sweeney Todd' c.1790)

Sweeney Todd, the 'Demon Barber of Fleet Street', was a
popular figure in the nineteenth-century penny
dreadfuls. The ghastly tale of his barber chair and the
human meat pies that its murderous mechanisms helped
contrive both shocked and fascinated generations of

Victorians. The original 'Sweeney Todd', however, was a
Parisian barber whose shop flourished in the Rue de la
Harpe shortly after the French Revolution. One day two
travellers arrived at the shop. They went in , leaving their
dog outside. The first traveller took a seat in the barber's
chair and asked for a shave. Rather than wait for his
friend, the other man went off on an errand. When he
returned ten minutes later there was no sign of his friend.
The barber announced that he had already left. His dog,
meanwhile, was still there, shivering, howling and refusing
to be moved. As the dog howled a crowd gathered and
tried to get into the shop, but the door had been locked.
Enraged, the mob smashed their way in and the dog leapt
on the barber, trying to tear his throat out. He was rescued
from its jaws, but when the crowd made their way to the
basement and found a hole through to the adjoining shop
he faced a far grimmer fate. There, in the next house, was
the body of the traveller, his throat cut, laid out on a table.
A quick check revealed that not only was this house owned
by one of Paris's leading *patissiers*, but that no one could
remember any meat ever being delivered to a shop from
which came meat pies with a superlative reputation.
Further searches revealed more bones and and some three
hundred skulls. The barber and the pie-maker were both
executed on the rack and the houses demolished. The
ground on which they stood was ordered to be kept
derelict for ever as a permanent reminder of evil.

Anselmi Albert and **Scalise** John
(beaten to death 1929)

For nearly ten years Anselmi and Scalise had served
Chicago gang-lord Al Capone as his leading trigger-men
and contract killers. Their scalps included Capone's rivals
Hymie Weiss and Dion 'Deanie' O'Bannion. They set new
standards for gangland assassinations – the first to
perpetrate the myth that garlic-rubbed bullets ensured a

deadlier kill, the inventors of the 'handshake kill', where
by one would grasp the victim's hand in a friendly greeting
while the other stepped up and shot the back of his head
off. But in 1929 an increasingly paranoid Capone decided
that his main men were no longer sufficiently loyal. On 7
May they were invited to a special dinner at the boss's
headquarters, the Hawthorn Hotel in Cicero, his
suburban fiefdom from whence he ruled Chicago.
Surrounded by their friends, jollied along by Capone
himself, the two killers ate their way through mounds of
linguine with shrimp sauce, washing it down with glasses
of Italian wine. Then, as short, fat, bald Anselmi and tall,
thin, squint-eyed Scalise relaxed in their chairs, Capone
summoned hidden assistants to tie up the two men.
Grasping a baseball bat, he walked up to his victims,
screaming accusations. Then, deliberately, one after the
other, the stocky gangster proceeded to smash each man's
unprotected skull to pulp with savage whirling blows from
the heavy wooden bat.

Atkins Charles *(lynched 1922)*

Fifteen-year-old Charles Atkins, a black youth living in
Davisboro, Ga., was arrested for the alleged murder of a
small shopkeeper, one Mrs Kitchens. Without waiting for
judge or jury, a mob of enraged Davisboro citizens took
the boy from the goal and proceeded to administer their
own perverted 'justice'. Atkins was held over a slow fire for
fifteen minutes and amid his shrieks of agony forced to
implicate a further black boy as an accomplice. The
ringleaders of the 2,000-strong mob chained Atkins to a
pine tree and built and lit a new fire around his legs. The
crazed rednecks then proceeded to empty two hundred
shots into his body, that provided, if nothing else, a release
from the flames.

Badger Harry *(died of careless eating)*

This famous Irish eccentric died as a result of a cruel
practical joke. Badger wore bizarre clothing – typically
yellow buckskin trousers, a bright red coat and a brass
helmet decorated with iron spikes – and in consequence
was treated as a suitable subject for ridicule and cruelty.
His other idiosyncrasy was a penchant for eating or
drinking whatever was put in front of him, regardless of its
nature. Jolly pranksters would pop a mouse into his beer
and he would innocently swig it down while they chortled
at their ingenuity. One day a merrymaker put before him a
dish of 'tripe' that consisted of strips of leather from a
huntsman's breeches, mixed with milk. Badger ate the
meal over a two-day period and died on the third day.

Bandera Stefan *(killed by a poison gun 1959)*

Bandera was a Ukrainian émigré living in Munich who was
dispatched by the KGB with a space-age weapon of the
kind one would expect to encounter in a paperback spy
thriller rather than real life. His murderer was Bogdan
Stashinsky, who had been specially trained in the use of a
harmless-looking metal tube, which was in reality a gun
devised to fire cyanide gas into a victim's face from short
range. Stashinsky simply walked up to Bandera as he was
opening his apartment door at 1 p.m. on 15 October 1959.
Bandera's corpse was discovered only five minutes later.

Barrow Eliza Mary *(poisoned 1911)*

Eliza Barrow, forty-nine, was poisoned by Frederick
Seddon in 1911 for an annuity of 65/- a week. The
unscrupulous and miserly Seddon, who was already
mulcting his victim as her greedy landlord, soaked the
arsenic from a threepenny packet of flypapers and used
the poison to dispatch his lodger. Then, to compound his
avarice, Seddon, who was district superintendent of the
London and Manchester Industrial Insurance Company,
arranged a pauper's funeral for his victim and took for his
pains a commission of 12/6 from the undertaker. He then
had issued memorial cards bearing the lines,

A dear one is missing and with us no more,
That voice so much loved we hear not again,
Yes we think of you now the same as of yore,
And know you are free from trouble and pain.

At his trial Seddon, a Mason, attempted to soften the
judge, a fellow Mason, by making a secret sign to him as he
summed up. The judge wept but still took the black cap.
Seddon was hanged in April 1912.

Bender Tony *(killed 1962)*

Bender was an American mobster whose real name was Anthony Strollo. He left his home for a brief walk on 8 April 1962 and was never seen again. The underworld account of his demise is that he was dumped into a cement mixer and is now part of a Manhattan skyscraper.

Bodasse Désiré

This 72-year-old retired French craftsman was killed for his money in 1868 by a political agitator and police spy named Voirbo. The latter, having killed the old man with a blow to the head from a flat iron, methodically set about distributing the body in a variety of resting places. He poured molten lead into the ears and threw the head into the river Seine from a bridge. He emptied the internal organs down a lavatory. He sewed the legs into bags of calico and lowered them into a well at the end of a cord; being questioned by two policemen while on his way to do this, he explained that the bags contained hams. He threw the remaining pieces of the body, cut into small bits, into the Seine from a basket, without any attempt at concealment. It was only when a neighbouring *restaurateur* noticed a sour taste in his water, and checked his well to find chunks of decaying human flesh polluting its contents, that the search and eventual arrest of Voirbo were set in motion. Voirbo never faced the full rigours of justice, but killed himself in his cell, cutting his throat with a concealed razor.

Brown Helen *(murdered 1937)*

Helen Brown was a 22-year-old waitress at Joe Ball's Sociable Inn in the small Texas town of Elmensdorf. She spent her days serving customers but, like most of Joe Ball's waitresses, her nights usually found her attending to the boss's more personal demands. Then, like four of her

predecessors at the Sociable Inn, Helen disappeared. As
far as Joe knew, she just upped and left without notice or
warning. The odd thing was, she hadn't taken any of her
clothes. Her mother, naturally, grew worried. Like
everyone else in town she had heard the rumours about
Joe and the waitresses, and she also knew about the
alligator pool behind the inn, where Joe kept his pets. It
was the pool that started investigations moving. After
Helen's mother contacted the Elmensdorf deputy sheriff,
policeman Elton Cude tried to take a look at the
foul-smelling pool. Before he could check on the
alligators, Joe Ball appeared, brandishing a shotgun. Cude
left, but he checked back later and found a rain barrel next
to the pool, in which were floating several hunks of bloody
flesh. He went to Ball and asked him about the meat. Just
'spoiled meat' for the alligators, he was told. But the net
was closing. An inquiry at the Elmensdorf bank revealed
that not only had Helen Brown left without her clothes,
she hadn't taken anything out of her bank account to cover
her trip either. Ball was arrested and questioned. The
police could not break him down until they tried a bluff:
Ball's handyman, they claimed, had told all. They took Ball
back to the Sociable Inn. He went behind the bar and
grabbed his shotgun again. This time, before police could
react, he turned it on himself and blew his head to bloody
pieces. The alligator meat was analysed and, sure enough,
it was human remains. With Joe dead, a neighbour,
hitherto too terrified to talk, appeared at the police station.
Some months before, he admitted, he had caught Joe Ball
butchering the body of a naked woman. Ball had
threatened to kill him if he betrayed the murder. The
neighbour had kept silent. But Helen Brown and four
other girls had died before the killer of the Sociable Inn
met his deserts.

Budd Grace *(killed and eaten 1928)*

Twelve-year-old Grace Budd found nothing sinister about silver-haired, grandfatherly Albert Fish, an apparently harmless old fellow who lived near her parents in Westchester County, New York, and who had persuaded them to let him take the youngster to a children's party he knew she would enjoy. But Grace and her parents were horribly wrong. Sixty-six-year-old Fish was far from a dear old fellow. He was a sadist, a masochist, a pervert of every excess, whose terrifying madness was to cost Grace Budd, among many other now unknown children, her life. Instead of making their way to the party, Fish and his young friend went to Wisteria Cottage, the quaintly named retreat where the sick old man enjoyed his grotesque indulgences. As she played quietly, Fish emerged, stark naked. When the girl screamed, Fish struck at her with a small kitchen cleaver, then grabbed her, strangled her to death and beheaded the corpse. Then he dismembered the body, stewing the flesh and organs with onions and carrots. Fish ate this appalling meal. When Grace failed to return, her parents – oddly it now seems – accepted her disappearance although they refused to believe she was dead. Not until six years had passed, and Fish, who had never returned to see them after he had consumed their daughter, wrote a letter confessing his crime, did they learn the truth.

Cabestan William de
(murdered and eaten thirteenth century)

Cabestan was a Provençal poet of the thirteenth century whose heart was cut out by a jealous competitor for the love of a lady and served up as a nicely dressed meal to the lady in question. The murderous chef was one Raymond de Seillans. The involuntarily cannibalistic young lady died of grief when she realised the true nature of her repast.

Churchman Leonard

(stabbed to death twentieth century)

Churchman was killed by being stabbed 124 times by his murderer, who went to the police and told them he had done it in self-defence.

Cole Thomas *(boiled to death twelfth century)*

Cole was the last of the sixty people murdered by the innkeeper Thomas Jarman and his wife at the Ostrich Inn in Colnbrook during the reign of Henry I. Travellers who seemed to be carrying considerable sums of money were

ushered by the Jarmans into a particular bedroom located over the large cellar in which the inn's beer was brewed. The bed in this room was set over a large trapdoor, and as soon as the unfortunate traveller was fast asleep the Jarmans would spring the bolts that held the trapdoor closed, so that the sleeper was tipped sideways out of bed straight into a huge cauldron of boiling water, causing instantaneous and silent death, apart from the splash. Cole was killed in this fashion, but the discovery of his wandering horse on the following day led to inquiries being made and revelation of the full history of the Jarmans' murderous activities.

Coleman Silas *(lynched 1936)*

Four Americans gathered with their wives at a cottage near Detroit for a weekend away from it all. As the weekend proceeded, the general feeling was that things were getting somewhat tedious. To remedy their boredom the eightsome lured into the cottage a black war veteran, one Silas Coleman. Telling him they needed to hire a wood carrier, they waited until he approached the lakeside retreat, then started shooting at the unsuspecting ex-soldier. Wounded, be began to run for shelter, and the party, all members of the racist Black Legion association, pursued him through the marshy land. When fishermen discovered the body some days later there were eighteen bullets embedded in it.

Constable Jean *(strangled twentieth century)*

Constable was strangled by a man who was sound asleep. The two had fallen asleep after a drinking party, lying together on a mattress on the floor. When the man woke up, he found that he had his hands around her throat and that she was already dead.

Cunningham John
(murdered while drunk twentieth century)

John Cunningham was an Australian down-and-out who, with three others, one an Aboriginal woman, started drinking 'a colossal amount of liquor' together in a rundown shack out in the bush. Sometime during the alcoholic orgy, the others turned against Cunningham and set about him. He was beaten with an iron bar and a lump of wood, kicked and punched, carved with a pocket knife and finally set alight after the woman poured kerosene over his unconscious body. Described as 'one of the most pathetic human beings in this state', the arsonist was jailed for eighteen months.

Davis Raymond Charles
(beaten to death twentieth century)

A harmless messenger boy had the misfortune to be chosen by a seventeen-year-old lunatic footman, Ernest Walker, as the victim of a murder as motiveless as the Leopold/Loeb killing of Bobbie Franks. Walker apparently decided that it would be fun to murder someone, so he waited until he had the house to himself, drew up a thirteen-item timetable for the murder and rang for a messenger boy to come round. After the deed had been done (with an iron bar), Walker departed, leaving a note for the butler which was headed, 'THE FATAL DAY - IN THE AFTERNOON' and began, 'I expect you will be surprised to see what I have done'.

Derer Herr *(died of human bite 1936)*

Innkeeper Derer of Elsbach, Bavaria, expected no special problems when he presented 24-year-old Oscar Zaettel with his bill for six quarts of beer. But it was, no doubt, this massive intake that made for the less than civilised reaction

from the customer. Protesting vehemently that he had
been overcharged, Zaettel turned on Derer, biting him
viciously in the neck. Infection set in and five days later the
unfortunate publican was dead. His assailant was gaoled
for three years.

Drago Pietro *(buried alive fifteenth century)*

Drago was a Milanese of the fifteenth century unfortunate
enough to earn the dislike of Duke Galeazzo Maria Sforza,
a tyrant famous for such pranks as starving a priest to
death, tying his favourite to a table and cutting off one of
his testicles, and forcing a peasant to kill himself by eating a
whole hare – bones, skin and all. Perhaps Drago was lucky;
all Sforza did to him was have him nailed up alive in a
coffin that he kept around the palace for some time before
burying it.

Durand-Deacon Olivia *(murdered 1949)*

Mrs Durand-Deacon's body was almost entirely dissolved
in a vat of sulphuric acid after having been shot in the head
by Haigh, the infamous 'acid bath' murderer, who wanted
her £40,000 fortune. All that remained of Mrs
Durand-Deacon after she had been converted to sludge
was 13 kg (30 lb) of body fat, parts of a heel bone, a pelvis,
an ankle and some false teeth. Since Haigh dispatched a
number of other victims in the same way, it is not entirely
certain that all the body fat belonged exclusively to Mrs
Durand-Deacon. None the less, those ascribable relics
were the evidence that sent this gruesome killer to the
gallows in August 1949.

Eupolis *(drowned fifth century BC)*

The misadventures at sea of this Greek comic poet at least
benefited other poets. First he was thrown into the sea by

Alcibiades on a journey to Sicily, in revenge for his having lampooned the sensitive statesman in one of his works. He survived this exercise in practical literary criticism, only to die in a shipwreck in the Hellespont a few years later. As a result of this, the Athenians passed a law prohibiting poets from serving abroad.

Germaine Deborah *(beaten to death)*

A nurse's aide in St Louis, Missouri, was bludgeoned to death with a 45 cm (18 in) plaster statuette of W. C. Fields. Perhaps the most astonishing aspect of this incident is the fact that such an object existed in the first place.

Gibson Eileen *(drowned 1947)*

Gibson, a fairly well known actress, was pushed into the Atlantic through the porthole of cabin 126 of the ocean liner *Durban Castle* on 18 October 1947. James Camb, a steward on the ship, was convicted of her murder even though her body was never recovered; it is not entirely clear just how she died, or indeed whether she was dead when pushed through the porthole. Camb's story was that she had unaccountably lapsed into unconsciousness during lovemaking. He said he had panicked when unable to resuscitate her and had seen the porthole as a ready solution to his dilemma.

Golding Joseph *(thrown to sharks twentieth century)*

Golding was thrown into shark-infested waters 112 kilometres (70 miles) from land by Michael Clark and Wyndham King, two fellow seamen on the SS *Camito* who objected to Golding's complaints about their drinking.

Gordon John *(scalded twentieth century)*

Gordon was killed in an RAOC camp in England by being pushed into a sterilising tank of boiling water by a kitchen hand with whom he was arguing about the possession of a small piece of bread and butter.

Gouffe *(seduced to death nineteenth century)*

Gouffe was victim of a deadly trick sprung on him, no doubt to his very great surprise, in the midst of what he took to be ingenious loveplay. Gouffe was the lover of a girl named Bompard in late-nineteenth-century Paris. Mlle Bompard, however, had another lover, named Eyraud, with whom she planned to murder and rob the amorous Gouffe. The latter was induced to sit in front of a curtain in an alcove of the girl's room. Mlle Bompard sat on his knee and playfully toyed with the infatuated Gouffe while Eyraud waited behind the curtain. Above Eyraud's head was a pulley from which hung a rope with a hook on the end. Mlle Bompard, in apparent playfulness, slipped a silken noose around Gouffe's neck, and at the same time passed the end to Eyraud behind the curtain. He immediately connected it to the hanging hook, pulled with all his might, and with the help of his pulley system hauled the astonished Gouffe up in the air, where he died of strangulation.

Gourier Pere *(ate to death eighteenth century)*

Gourier, a rich landowner in eighteenth-century France, delighted in murder, but only of the most bizarre and utterly legal kind. He ate his victims into their graves. He would invite a man to a series of massive and richly cooked restaurant meals, always picking up the bill, always making sure the victim accepted a new invitation as soon as the current feast had been choked down. Sooner or later – and few could hold out for more than a couple of months –

Gourier's chosen involuntary gluttons perished – usually
of heart attacks as the massive *gourmandise* took its toll.
Gourier met his match when he turned on one Ameline, a
second assistant to the public executioner of Paris. The
routine began as ever. The duo toured the various palaces
of *haute cuisine*, Ameline eating, Gourier eating, and
picking up the bills. Occasionally Ameline broke the ritual
by leaving Paris for a few days. He told his new-found
friend that he was officiating in various provincial
executions but, tipped off by a waiter friend who had seen
Gourier at work before, Ameline was actually rushing off
to a secret hideout to fast and purge himself of all that rich
intake. When his victim lasted an unprecedented twelve
months, Gourier redoubled his efforts. When two years
were notched up, he fed him even harder, and all the time

ate plate for plate, as Ameline seemed proof against the most luscious, cholesterol-filled meals. In the end irony prevailed. Tucking into an enormous steak, both men had reached their fourteenth slice of the massive sirloin. As his victim speared yet another piece of meat, Gourier turned red, then stark white. Ameline paused, hearing what he thought was a sneeze. But it was not. Gourier's death rattle was his final gesture as he slumped into his plate, prone across his terminal blow-out.

Greenfield Alfred *(stabbed and mutilated 1961)*

A Sydney derelict had the misfortune to be the first known victim of the so-called Mutilator, William McDonald, who terrorised Sydney in the early 1960s. The Mutilator (it was never entirely clear whether his name really was McDonald, since he used more than one alias) specialised in stabbing derelicts to death by night and then mutilating their genital organs. His victims, of whom there were at least four, were all men; he stated later that they reminded him of a British army corporal who had indecently assaulted him.

Gutteridge PC George *(shot 1927)*

This Essex policeman was shot dead in September 1927 by Frederick Browne, a petty thief. As Gutteridge lay dead, staring up at Browne with sightless eyes, Browne deliberately shot him twice more, sending a bullet through each eye. This was apparently done because of Browne's fear that his image would somehow be retained upon the dead man's eyes.

Hawle *(lynched 1378)*

A man of this name, who had escaped from the Tower of London, was killed in Westminster Abbey during Mass in

1378. With a fellow-prisoner named Shackle he had been chased into the abbey by the Constable of the Tower and Sir Ralph Ferrers, together with no fewer than fifty armed men. Just as the deacon was reading the gospel of the day, Hawle and Shackle burst into the abbey with their fifty-two pursuers at their heels. Hawle ran twice around the choir, his enemies cutting at him with their swords as he ran, until he sank dead in front of the prior's stall. In recognition of this unheard-of desecration of the abbey, Hawle was buried within the abbey and the spot where he fell was marked with a brass effigy.

Hewson Tom *(drowned fourteenth century)*

Hewson was a fourteenth-century drummer boy who was killed by being pushed into a deep well behind the church at Harpham in Yorkshire by the local squire. Hewson's mother was said to be a witch. There was later a local tradition that deaths among families descended from the squire have been foreshadowed by drumbeats coming from the depths of the well.

Kaye Emily *(murdered 1924)*

Murdered and dismembered by the ladykiller Patrick Mahon in 1924, Miss Kaye succeeded in terrifying and ultimately convicting her murderer *after her dismemberment*. Mahon had killed her in a lonely cottage, where he proceeded to cut off her legs and head. He started a fire in the living room and at midnight placed Miss Kaye's head upon it. At precisely that moment, a loud clap of thunder shook the house and, as the head sat on the glowing coals, its eyes opened. Presumably this was due to the effect of heat on the eyelids, but a terrified Mahon fled into the night. Later, when he was being tried for murder, he put up a confident front until, just as his own lawyer asked him a crucial question, there was a flash of lightning and a violent clap of thunder. Mahon shrank back into a corner of the witness box in abject fear, a broken man. He was convicted and executed.

Kelly Mary *(murdered 1888)*

Like the four previous victims of Jack the Ripper, Mary Kelly was an East End prostitute. She lived in a common lodging house at 26 Dorset Street, where she occupied room number 13 for a rent of four shillings (20p) a week. On 9 November 1888, Mary Kelly's life was grim. She was three months pregnant, but her common-law husband Joseph Barnett had deserted her after she resented his bringing home another woman, also a whore, to sleep with them. She owed three months' rent for which her landlord was dunning her. What money she had came from soliciting in the mean streets of the East End. Mary Kelly's last night alive started in a pub in nearby Commercial Street. She left the pub, according to eyewitnesses, at around 11.45 p.m. Her companion was a stout man in shabby clothes, with a carroty moustache and a blotchy face. As she left she drunkenly informed the world that she would have a 'little sing' and launched into 'Only a violet I plucked from my mother's grave when a boy'. She was still in a maudlin mood when neighbours heard her arrive home at 1 a.m. At about 3.30 a.m. the resident of room 20, another working girl, heard cries of 'Murder!' but did nothing. Such cries were common enough around Dorset Street. At 10.45 the following morning Mary's landlord remembered her arrears and sent his assistant Thomas Bowyer to see what she had to offer. Bowyer knocked on the door, but there was no reply. Then he stared through a broken window to see if she was asleep. The sight that greeted his eyes sent him running for a policeman. Mary Kelly had been brutally, obscenely murdered. Her remains lay on the bed. Her heart lay on the pillow, her breasts on a table, and her entrails had been draped over a picture frame. Experts worked out that the Ripper had taken two hours to complete his savage surgery. The contemporary *Illustrated Police News* reported the mutilations:

The throat had been cut right across with a knife, nearly severing the head from the body. The abdomen had been partially ripped open, and both breasts had been cut from the body, the left arm, like the head, hung to the body by skin only. The nose had been cut off, the forehead skinned, and the thighs, down to the feet, stripped of the flesh. The abdomen had been slashed with a knife across, downwards and the liver and entrails wrenched away. The entrails and other portions of the frame were missing, but the liver etc., it is said, were found placed between the feet of this poor victim. The flesh from the thighs and legs, together with the breasts and nose, had been placed by the murderer on the table, and one of the hands of the dead woman had been pushed into her stomach.

Lancelin Madame and Geneviève
(beaten to death 1933)

The Lancelins, mother and daughter, were murdered in the French provincial town of Le Mans in 1933 by their two maids, the sisters Christine and Lea Papin. The two murderesses attributed their act to the frustration they had experienced when the electric iron had blown out twice in three days. They said that the Lancelins had on occasions been somewhat demanding, testing the quality of the maids' dusting by rubbing white-gloved fingers over the dusted surfaces, etc. Still, this is hardly sufficient to account for the sheer savagery with which Madame Lancelin and Geneviève were killed. The first indication of the crime was given when two policemen, walking upstairs in the dark and using a flashlight (the faulty iron had blown the house lights too), came across a single eye on the third step from the landing. On the landing itself were the two bodies, their heads smashed in, their thighs notched with knife-cuts and their fingernails rooted out. One of

Geneviève's teeth had been hammered into her head. Another single eye lay nearby. The elder of the two murderous sisters, Christine, seems to have been the instigator and during her imprisonment and trial displayed some remarkable characteristics. She struggled her way out of a straitjacket, had hallucinations and jumped to the top of a barred window three metres (9 ft 8 in) up and hung there for some time in an astonishing feat of strength.

Leonard Oliver *(poisoned twentieth century)*

Leonard was poisoned with phosphorus by the lady he had only just married – a Mrs Wilson, whose previous husband Ernest had also died within a few days of his wedding. When Leonard died, suspicion was aroused by the memory of a remark Mrs Wilson had made at the reception. When a guest commented on the quantity of cakes and sandwiches left over, Mrs Wilson said, 'Just keep them for the funeral, although I might give this one a week's extension.'

M'Guire *(impaled on a poker 1894)*

This woman was killed in 1894 by a man named Paterson who thrust a red-hot poker up her vagina, penetrating the peritoneal cavity.

Malloy Mike *(murdered by multiple methods 1933)*

For those who needed hard-won dollars at the height of the American Depression, normal standards of behaviour were often soon abandoned. In spring 1932 five men formed a strange syndicate. Tony Marino, a speakeasy owner, and four of his customers — Dan Kreisberg, a fruit seller, Frank Pasqua, an undertaker, Joseph Murray, Marino's bartender, and Harry Green, a cabbie – banded

together as the poor man's Murder Incorporated. They
planned to insure people and then kill them, after which
they would collect on the policy. The first plan went well
enough. A woman friend of Marino's, a well-known
drinker, was taken when soused to her room. There she
was stripped, soaked with water and left with icy winds
blowing through the open windows. She duly contracted
pneumonia, and Marino and the boys pulled in $800
worth of insurance. In 1933 they turned to another
hard-drinking customer – a down-and-out alcoholic
named Mike Malloy, aged sixty and apparently hanging
on to life by the slimmest of threads. Secretly the syndicate
took out a policy worth $3,576 on Malloy, collectible if he
died in an accident. There then began an amazing
catalogue of some thirty murder attempts on the hapless
tramp. To start with, Malloy was fed antifreeze instead of
his usual rotgut bourbon as he sat in the speakeasy. He
downed six shots, then keeled over. The conspirators were
rejoicing when he lurched to his feet, apologised for
falling over and asked for a fresh drink. Further attempts
to alter his drinking habits included shots of turpentine,
horse liniment, rat poison, spoiled raw oysters and straight
wood alcohol. But Malloy just kept coming back for more.
The killers changed from drink to food. A daunting
concoction of sardines, wood shavings, tacks and general
garbage was served up as a 'sandwich'. Malloy gobbled it
up, poured a couple of shots of 'bourbon' (this time wood
alcohol) after it and still lived. Then they tried the freezing
trick. After Malloy had passed out – as usual – they
dumped him half naked in a local park. Five gallons of
water were poured over his recumbent form and he was
left to die in the 14° Fahrenheit cold. Unsurprisingly,
Malloy survived this too. Then, passed out as ever, Malloy
was dumped in the street, and Harry Green drove his taxi
at 45 mph (70 kph) over the helpless hobo. This time they
were sure he was dead. But three weeks later Malloy
stumbled through the barroom doors. He apologised for

his absence but someone had knocked him down and he'd been in hospital with brain concussion and a fractured shoulder. Finally they took his unconscious form up to bartender Murray's apartment. Here they stuck a rubber hose, into his mouth, the other end connected to a gas pipe. They turned on the gas jet. This time, finally, Malloy was dead. But his killers did not enjoy their success long. The police were soon suspicious about this death. They checked on Malloy's drinking buddies and arrested them. Marino, Pasqua and Kreisberg all died in the electric chair at Sing Sing.

Maranzano Salvatore

Inventor of the term *cosa nostra* ('this thing of ours'), Maranzo was an American gangster who was done to death in September 1931 in a way that suggested his killers were taking no chances. He was strangled, his throat cut, stabbed six times and finally shot, four bullets being subsequently found in his head and body.

Markov Georgy *(killed by poison gun 1978)*

Markov was a Bulgarian émigré who was murdered in London in 1978 by someone who injected a tiny metal ball containing a minute quantity of poison into his thigh while he waited at a bus stop with a group of other people. The metal ball had a hole in it containing the ricin, plugged up with wax. The heat of Markov's body dissolved this, releasing the ricin. The murderer apparently bumped into Markov with his umbrella and apologised politely before disappearing in the busy street. At first it was thought the umbrella itself had been the murder weapon; later it was considered more likely that the killer had used it as a screen for the real weapon, a syringe of some kind. (Ricin is the poisonous substance in the leaves of the castor oil tree.)

Murray Lavinia and **Barnes** Sheila
(victims of a cannibal 1958)

Two five-year-old girls made the mistake of wandering into the house of the 71-year-old lunatic Tom Burns while he was playing the piano. Their bodies were drained of blood and parts were cooked and eaten.

North Simon *(drowned eighteenth century)*

North was killed by eighteenth-century gamblers to settle a bet. North was unlucky enough to be nearby when a high-living young rake bet a group of friends that a man could live under water. They immediately seized North, put him in a caulked and sealed barrel and lowered it into the waters of a lake. The barrel was watertight but contained inadequate oxygen. When North was hauled to the surface, the gambler had lost his bet. Not to be deterred, he tried again – this time the victim was fortunate and survived, and the gambler recouped what he had lost on North.

Nurayana *(killed by a cricket stump 1933)*

Nurayana, playing as wicket-keeper for a team in Mysore, India, was killed when a fast ball shattered one of the stumps behind which he crouched. The seventeen-year-old student died when the metal 'shoe' at the point of the stump pierced his heart and, although probably not fatally, the ball struck him in the eye. Forty-three years later, in Pakistan, an umpire so enraged the members of the fielding side, against whom he gave a number of controversial decisions, that they abandoned the game, broke down the wicket and beat him to death with the stumps.

Ohama Matsuzo *(executed 1974)*

In August 1974 Matsuzo Ohama, a 48-year-old architect,
infuriated beyond reason by the constant piano playing
from a neighbouring apartment, killed a mother and her
two daughters to silence their noise. At his trial Ohama
asked for a capital sentence since only through death could
he ever achieve the silence he craved. The court accepted
his plea and Ohama was duly hanged for his murders.

O'Hara Bridie *(strangled 1965)*

A 28-year-old prostitute was the last of six female victims
of a man who had a penchant for *fellatio*, in the inner
western suburbs of London over a period of twelve

months from February 1964 to February 1965. All were strangled or suffocated while in a kneeling position over the killer's lap and their gullets showed evidence of the nature of the activity in which they had been engaged. The aspect that renders these deaths particularly appalling is that there was evidence, in at least one case, that death had been caused by asphyxiation when the killer's penis obstructed the victim's windpipe.

Parkman Dr George *(murdered 1850)*

Parkman was last seen alive entering the laboratory of his fellow-professor, John W. Webster, in Boston, in order to obtain repayment of some money he had lent Webster. When Parkman's absence from his usual haunts became apparent, his friends called in the police. The latter searched Webster's laboratory, where they found the haunch bones, a thigh and a leg of an adult. In Webster's furnace they found skull fragments and artificial teeth and in a tea-chest they found the trunk of a human body and another thigh. Put together, these relics clearly constituted the remains of the unwary debt collector. The prosecution's expert witness at Webster's trial was the famous lawyer Oliver Wendell Holmes.

Paterson Mary *(murdered 1828)*

Paterson was a particularly beautiful Edinburgh prostitute who was murdered in 1828 by Burke and Hare so that they could sell her cadaver to the surgeons for dissection. After killing her, they carried the body through the streets of Edinburgh in broad daylight to take it to one Dr Knox. Children followed them, chanting, 'They are carrying a corpse.' Her body was so beautiful that Dr Knox preserved it in whisky for three months before dissecting it. He paid £10 for the body, and probably as much for the whisky.

When Mary Paterson was laid out for dissection, some of the students recognised her and artists came to study and sketch her.

Pickles Susan *(strangled 1957)*

This baby was strangled in England in 1957 by her 21-year-old babysitter because her crying interrupted a radio programme to which the babysitter wanted to listen.

Pucci, Oracio *(hanged sixteenth century)*

Pucci was hanged from the very same bar of the very same window in the Palazzio Vecchio from which his father was hanged. In each case the perpetrator of the deed was Francesco I, the sixteenth-century Florentine tyrant.

Rebet Lev *(killed by poison gun 1957)*

This Ukranian émigré in Munich earned the dubious distinction of being murdered by a technique that would not have been out of place in a James Bond thriller. The KGB agent Stashinsky (who subsequently defected and revealed all) shot him in the face with a spray of cyanide vapour from a special gun in the form of a metal tube, while casually passing him on a staircase.

Reese Anna May *(blown up twentieth century)*

Ms Reese was dynamited from below while in bed making love with her boyfriend. Her estranged husband had put a stick of dynamite between the mattress and the bed springs and had run a fuse from it through a loose board to a spot outside the house. He waited with his ear to the wall until he heard Anna May in bed with her lover, then he lit the fuse. Apparently the lovers did not hear any sound of the fuse burning, and, when the explosion took place, Anna May's boyfriend was on top of her; he escaped with nothing more serious than burned hands.

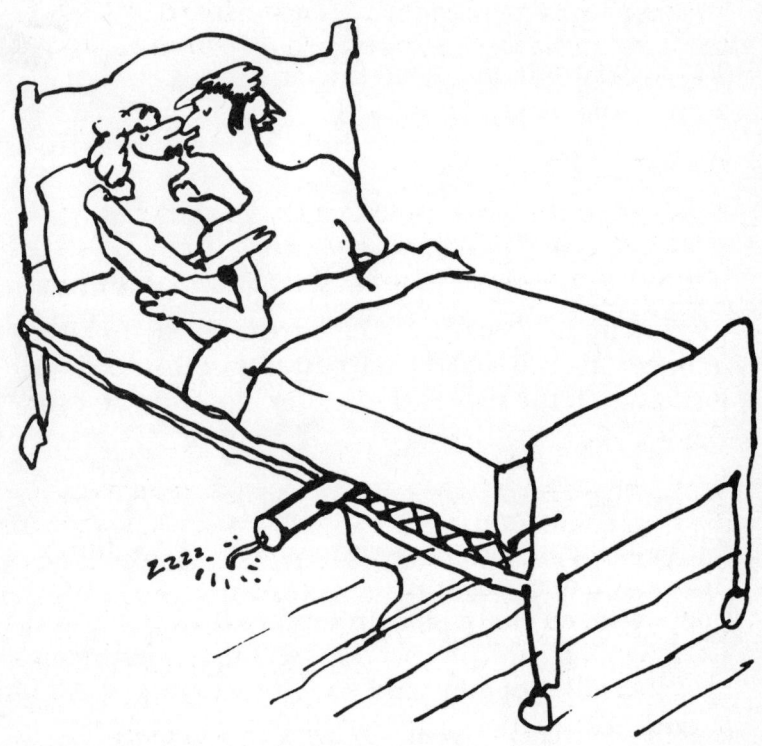

Reles Abe *('fell' to his death 1941)*

A chubby and jovial American gunman, also known as 'Kid Twist', was involved in many slayings for Murder Incorporated. He turned canary and sang to the police, giving details of hundreds of crimes, including numerous murders, and incriminating many of his former associates. Reles died when he mysteriously fell from the window of a sixth-floor hotel room while being guarded – by *eighteen* policemen.

Robinson Rose *(strangled twentieth century)*

Mrs Robinson achieved the dubious distinction of being strangled by a man with no fingers. As the result of an accident, the murderer had only short stumps where his fingers should have been. This made his so unlikely a suspect that police at first refused to believe he was responsible.

Rosse Richard *(boiled 1530)*

This sixteenth-century cook was boiled to death at Smithfield in 1530 as punishment for having poisoned some gruel he was making for the Bishop of Rochester's household.

Rothe Friedel
(bitten to death, then sold as sausages 1919)

Rothe, along with fifty other unfortunate German youths, died at the hands of the homosexual cannibal killer Fritz Haarmann. Born in 1879, Haarmann had lived a life of petty crime – from thieving to indecent exposure – and in 1918, after a more than usually protracted spell in gaol, opened a cookshop in Hamburg's old quarter. His shop soon became popular, both for its tasty products and for the simple fact that here, apparently, was meat in abundance despite the general lack of such luxuries in post-First World War Germany. The truth behind the flavoursome cooking was hideous. Haarmann, aided by his sidekick, one Hans Gans, who allegedly helped only for the pick of the victim's clothing, lured young men from the railway stations and alleys back to his apartment where he offered them sex and a bed for the night. Rothe, like many others, was destitute and all too glad to accommodate the older man in return for food and comfort. Instead Haarmann bit him through the throat, and he died from loss of blood. His body was then butchered and, before

long, Haarmann's restaurant was serving up another
plateful of tasty sausages. Not until 1924, when
Haarmann's tally had reached some fifty victims, was
Rothe, not to mention his fellow victims, avenged. He was
executed for his crimes that same year. Gans served twelve
years in gaol.

Rudnick George 'Whitey'
(stabbed, beaten and strangled twentieth century)

Rudnick was an American loan-shark killed by gangsters.
His killers stabbed him no fewer than sixty-three times
with an ice pick and knives, smashed his skull and
strangled him as well.

Scalise Joe *(slashed to death 1957)*

This American gangster unwisely accepted an invitation to
a party at the home of one of his enemies, Jimmy 'Jerome'
Squillante, a garbage collection racketeer. When Scalise
arrived he was carved up with butchers' knives and sent on
his way as packed garbage in one of Squillante's garbage
trucks.

Schultz Dutch *(shot 1935)*

Schultz, whose real name was Arthur Fliegenheimer, was
an American mobster who specialised in beer racketeering
in New York. Like many of his kind, Schultz had come up
the hard way, killing, bombing and hijacking; but unlike
his peers, who realised by 1935 that their operations
needed less publicity and more cunning, he never wanted
to give up his old ways. When crusading official Thomas
Dewey started cracking down on the mobs, Schultz's
immediate response was to order him killed. His fellow
syndicate members – Lucky Luciano, Vito Genovese and
the other bosses – vetoed such mad-dog excess. Instead, it

was decreed, the mad dog himself must be silenced. On 23 October 1935, as Schultz sat with three friends in the Palace Chop House and Tavern in Newark, New Jersey, Charlie 'the Bug' Workman entered and machine-gunned all four diners. Schultz died in Newark City Hospital as a confession-hungry police stenographer recorded his surreal stream of final words. The tirade ended with a plea: 'Let them leave me alone.' Then the Dutchman fell silent and died.

Semple George *(pushed off a cliff 1960)*

A three-year-old boy was pushed over the edge of a high cliff near Brighton by a family friend. The latter, a middle-aged woman, was taking him for a walk and sent him plunging to his death because, she said, 'He would not behave.'

Simpson Abigail *(murdered 1827)*

The first female victim of the notorious bodysnatchers Burke and Hare. Suffocated, stripped and packed in a tea-chest, she was taken at once by a hired porter to the surgeon Dr Knox, who not only failed to question the provenance of the body that he was buying but also complimented Burke and Hare on its freshness.

Skalky Julius *(pushed under subway 1976)*

Julius Skalky, a New York printer, was waiting for his subway train when he was suddenly grabbed from behind by one Richard Pratt, aged forty-three. Pratt, whom Skalky, it was later ascertained, had never met, proved to be an inmate of an upstate mental hospital out on temporary leave. This information came too late to save Skalky, who was dragged to the edge of the platform and pushed under the oncoming train as a crowd of shocked and immobile passengers watched him go to his death.

Spinks Mary *(poisoned 1897)*

A London alcoholic was poisoned with antimony by George Chapman, one of the prime suspects for the Jack the Ripper killings. Had she known, it might have been some consolation to her that the antimony preserved her body wonderfully after death. Sir Thomas Stevenson, who exhumed her body after five years, wrote:

On opening the coffin, a female body was disclosed of an almost lifelike aspect, except for the pallor of the countenance, which was covered with a fine mealy deposit of earthy phosphates, giving the appearance of the face having been dusted with face-powder. There was no putrefactive odour. There were no larvae in or around the body. The short, dark hair of the head was clean and unchanged. The fingers and hands were of a pink colour. No fungi were visible on the surface of the body.

The foregoing appearances are all the more remarkable when it is realised that the coffin in which Spinks was buried was at the bottom of a public grave 6 metres (18 ft) deep, that seven other coffins had been deposited in the grave on top of it and that the stench from the other coffins was terrible.

Squillante Jimmy 'Jerome' *(crushed to death 1960)*

An American racketeer *(see* Scalise, Joe) who disappeared in 1960; according to the underworld grapevine, he was loaded into the boot of a car that was then put into a crushing machine that compacted it into a cube of scrap metal for melting down in a blast furnace.

Thomas Julia *(killed, cooked and sold 1879)*

Mrs Thomas, of Hammersmith, London, was murdered with an axe by her housekeeper Kate Webster. Her dismembered remains were boiled in a copper by the thrifty housekeeper, who made what she could out of a bad business by selling the victim's false teeth (for six shillings) and two jars of 'best dripping'. The unsaleable residue, including Mrs Thomas' head, was thrown into the Thames.

Vincent Christopher *(drowned twentieth century)*

A five-week-old baby was taken from his pram in a crowded shopping centre by a passing lunatic who was on leave from a mental hospital and thrown into the River Wye.

Wagner Evelyn *(burnt to death 1973)*

One October night in 1973 the manager of a shop in Melbourne saw an appalling sight. A woman, her entire body on fire, walked calmly into his shop to request, 'Will you please call an ambulance', and then walked out just as calmly. 'It was amazing,' the storeman said later. 'Her face was blazing, her clothes were smouldering, her skin was peeling.' The woman died four hours later, hideously burnt. Police inquiries ascertained that she had been carrying a can of petrol for her stalled car when she was attacked by a group of young men who dragged her behind an apartment block, forced her to drench herself with the petrol and then simply tossed a lighted match on to her. They walked off. Neither robbery nor sexual assault was involved.

Willats Fleetwood *(poisoned 1919)*

Willats was killed by an unbelievably cruel practical joke. He was a lonely old man who, on his way home from the local pub, met two strangers and entered into conversation with them. He drank about two tablespoons of some whisky they offered him, but, since it tasted more like a sweet wine of some kind, he declined any more. Next day he was taken ill, and died in hospital. The post-mortem showed that he had swallowed a small quantity – about two tablespoonsful – of hydrochloric acid.

Zwillman Abner 'Longy' *('strangled' himself 1959)*

Zwillman had been a long-time associate of top gangster Meyer Lansky, but by 1959, aged seventy, their friendship had grown less binding. Zwillman was found hanging in the basement of his own house. He had supposedly taken a length of plastic cord and killed himself. It was hard, even for the most blinkered, to discount two factors: one, the heavy bruising on Zwillman's body and, two, the fact that despite his 'suicide', his hands were securely tied together with wire. And, as contemporaries pointed out, if Longy had really wanted to end it all, his particular line of business kept him in enough guns to end it rather more simply than with such Houdini-esque contortions.

All in
the family

Abercrombie Helen *(murdered 1830)*

The twenty-year-old sister-in-law of her poisoner, artist
Thomas Griffiths Wainewright, Abercrombie died
because her thick ankles offended the killer's sense of
artistic proportion. The life insurance policy worth
£18,000 that she had taken out may have helped his sense
of taste.

Amin Kay *(garrotted 1970s)*

Having come into disfavour with her husband, General
Amin of Uganda, Kay Amin was garrotted. But this was
only the beginning. Her relatives were summoned and
compelled to observe her body being dismembered and
the various parts – legs, arms and head – sewn back on
again in wrong places for the General's entertainment.
The medical attendant who was forced to perform this
ghastly operation had a nervous breakdown.

Anonymous American Male *(shot 1981)*

A married couple from Dallas, Texas, were arguing
bitterly over who might have shot 'J.R.', the villain of the
television show *Dallas*. So enraged did the wife become
that, with a gesture worthy of the soap opera itself, she
waited only until the credits rolled before taking out the
family shotgun and killing her husband. A nephew said

later that she had been 'under strain' for some time. To what degree this was centred on her favourite TV show was not specified.

Anonymous Californian boy *(shot 1958)*

Two brothers lived in Pasadena, California. The elder was nothing if not kooky. For his last two years at the local high-school he persisted in hiding his eyes – either shielding them, as if from the sun, when one hand was free, or adopting a black 'Lone Ranger' mask when two hands were required, for sport and similar activities. One day in 1958 the younger brother was alone in the bathroom. Stepping outside the door he was confronted by his brother, brandishing a pistol he had obtained through a mail order firm. Before the youngster could speak, his elder brother shot him. The boy fell back inside, managing to slam the door behind him. He lay inside for several minutes as his elder brother begged and pleaded, interspersing tears with entreaties and apologies – promising that it was all a mistake, and *please*, would he just come out. Finally, mollified, if still shocked and confused, the young boy opened the door once more. His brother raised the gun once more and this time riddled him with shots until the corpse lay inert and bloodsoaked before him. Interviewed in custody later that night, the 'Lone Ranger', who for a while had paraded the touch-lines cheering on his high-school football team, explained why he had felt it necessary to keep his eyes covered all those years: 'They lacked lustre,' he remarked.

Anonymous West German male *(stabbed 1975)*

After eating strawberries in bed an unnamed German foolishly wiped his messy hands on the marital sheets. Appalled by such slovenliness, his 59-year-old wife picked up a kitchen knife and stabbed him in the recently filled stomach. He died without leaving his bed.

Barlow Elizabeth *(murdered 1957)*

Barlow, an English housewife, was murdered in 1957 by the injection of a massive dose of 15,000 units of insulin. This unusual if not unique method of dispatch was chosen by her husband, Kenneth, a former nurse, in the belief that detection would be impossible. Not so. The doctor attending the death noticed hypodermic puncture marks on Mrs Barlow's buttocks, and tests revealed evidence of insulin in the flesh around the injection marks.

Bartlett Edwin *(murdered 1886)*

Bartlett was the clichéd Victorian eccentric, whose impeccable exterior masked some less predictable personality traits. For eleven years his marriage to an expatriate Frenchwoman, Adelaide, had been based on Bartlett's own concept of the institution. A man, he felt, should be allowed two wives: one for 'use' and one for a companion. Adelaide Bartlett found herself in the second category, although she had no evidence that her husband was showing any interest in finding a more 'useful' partner. In 1885 the Bartletts met a young Wesleyan minister, the Reverend George Dyson. He was a regular visitor to their home, and the conversation often turned to Edwin's view of marriage. It was during these chats that Edwin assured both his wife and the clergyman that his dearest wish was that after his death the two of them should be united in matrimony. He wanted, as he put it, 'to give' Adelaide to the minister. As a rehearsal for such posthumous fulfilment, he would encourage them to kiss and would watch spellbound as they embraced to order. Dyson was bewildered but more than happy to enjoy the attractive Frenchwoman. He wrote her naïve poems, calling her 'queenlike' and 'My Birdie'. On New Year's Day 1886, Edwin Bartlett was found dead in bed at the Pimlico lodgings the couple were using. A post-mortem proved he had been killed by swallowing chloroform. What astounded the experts was that while only a few drops of chloroform held under the nose could kill, Edwin Bartlett had swallowed, or had been forced to swallow, a whole bottle. Police inquiries proved that Dyson had been buying the drug from various chemists shortly before Bartlett's demise, but Adelaide swore that the drug was part of Edwin's nightly anaesthetic. For Edwin, hitherto so quiescent, had suddenly revealed an interest in his wife that after eleven years was more than merely companionable. The mystery remains: whether Edwin Bartlett was murdered, killed himself or simply took the drug by mistake, how was it possible for him to swallow so much of the burning liquid? As Sir James Paget, the investigating surgeon, remarked after Adelaide had been acquitted; 'Now she's acquitted, she should tell us, in the interests of science, how she did it.'

Barton Roy *(knifed 1977)*

Roy Barton married his wife Tina without worrying that thirty-three years before her mother had been tried and found guilty of knifing to death her father. Theirs was not a happy marriage. Unable to conceive, Tina filled the house with dolls and dogs to make up for the lack of offspring. On April Fool's Day 1977 they argued fiercely. He called her 'a childless bitch' and 'the daughter of a whore and a murderess', then dared her to kill him, boasting that she could never do it as he came from Invercargill, the world's most southern city, 'and you can't kill an Invercargill man!' Undeterred, Tina Barton stabbed her husband thirty-six times in the heart. Tried for murder in the same Christchurch, New Zealand, court where her mother was condemned, Tina was convicted only of manslaughter, after a jury felt she had been provoked by her husband's braggadocio.

Benn Rev. Julius *(battered to death twentieth century)*

Benn was murdered by his insane son, William, whose choice of a weapon must surely be unique. The Reverend Julius was battered to death with a chamberpot. The author's sources do not reveal whether it was full or empty at the time.

Bennett John G. *(shot 1929)*

John Bennett and his wife Myrtle, of Kansas City, were both bridge fanatics. They played continually, with dedication that went right over the top into obsession. Thus when they fell out, the arguments were vehement. One night, as their opponents watched with increasing embarrassment, they duly fell out over cards. John accused Myrtle of overbidding, at which point she accused him of being a 'bum bridge player'. At this point he slapped her face. Myrtle promptly left the table. She vanished into the bedroom, but not for a therapeutic cry. She returned at once, brandishing a revolver. Their marital quarrel concluded when she shot him dead across the card table. At her trial she was acquitted of murder. Alexander Woollcott, the American writer and broadcaster, claimed in a story that years later Myrtle Bennett was again at the bridge table. When her partner made a blunder and remarked, quite innocently, 'You'll shoot me for this', the former Mrs Bennett fainted clean away.

Blot Mlle *(killed by mother 1928)*

When Mlle Blot, a 21-year-old Rouen girl, informed her mother she was leaving home for Paris and an independent life, her mother was less than acquiescent. Convinced that a life in Paris was tantamount to the grossest immorality, she forbade her daughter even to consider such a move. Mlle Blot persisted, informing her mother that she was old enough to know her own mind, and Madame produced a revolver and summarily put an end to her daughter's plan, and indeed her life. A tragic figure in the dock, Madame Blot was acquitted of murder.

Boia Dunawd *(throat cut)*

A Welsh maiden of olden times was killed in appalling circumstances upon St David's Peninsula in Pembrokeshire. Her stepmother took her into the forest to gather nuts and, when they had reached a secluded spot, persuaded her to rest awhile. She then suggested that Dunawd should place her head in her stepmother's lap to have her hair combed. Dunawd did this, whereupon her throat was cut.

Borowski Joseph *(mutilated twentieth century)*

Sixty-six-year-old Joseph Borowski died in his Chicago apartment during a two-month spell of blizzards that effectively cut off the building from the outside world. Marooned and without food, his 61-year-old widow Maria tried to keep alive by eating his flesh. When police finally broke in and found Maria dead, they also found Joseph's legs, cut off at the knee, in a box, his intestines wrapped in brown paper in the freezer and other parts of his body lying about the house, wrapped up in neat little packages.

Bromley Mrs William, Ian and Richard

In February 1974, as Edward Heath's government fell under the pressure of the three-day week and similar industrial disruption in England, Dr William Bromley placed a message on the telephone-answering service in his surgery: 'As it now appears that the Labour Party will get in, I can see no point in living.' He then shot dead his wife and two young sons, aged respectively nine and four.

He stopped short at suicide, but faced no trial and was committed to a mental hospital for an indefinite period.

Brown Archibald *(murdered 1943)*

Mr Brown of Rayleigh, Essex, was a regular tyrant around his middle-class home. His wife and two sons, Eric and Colin, had learnt to do what father said or fear his wrath. Most of his anger was aimed at Eric, nineteen, who was currently in the army and whom he had persecuted ever since boyhood. In 1938, five years earlier, Mr Brown had suffered an accident which had left him paralysed from the waist down. It hadn't improved his tyrannical temper either. A nurse, Miss Mitchell, was hired, and every day she would put Mr Brown into his velveteen upholstered bath chair, settle cushions and blankets and take him off for his constitutional. On 23 July 1943, Nurse Mitchell prepared her patient as usual. She helped him into his bath chair, adjusted his cushions, tucked in the blankets, and off they went. This time Mr Brown's afternoon walk came to a sudden end. Nurse and patient had gone only a short distance when a British Army Hawkins No. 75 grenade mine, which had been placed in the upholstery of the chair, exploded. Nurse Mitchell was blown off her feet but survived. The autocratic Mr Brown had issued his last order. He was blown to pieces, mingled in death with the debris of his bath chair. It took no time to discover the culprit. Nurse Mitchell recalled how Eric, who was on leave, was constantly pottering around the air-raid shelter where the chair was stored. A check with his regiment proved that he had easy access to the Hawkins grenades. Eric soon confessed, saying: 'My father is now out of his suffering and I earnestly hope that my mother will now live a much happier and more normal life.' Diagnosed as a chronic schizophrenic, Eric was found guilty but insane.

Bryan Pearl *(murdered 1896)*

Pearl was killed and decapitated by her lover Scott Jackson and a dental student named Alonzo Walling, in Kentucky. The killers got rid of the head, but forensic pathologists were able to deduce from the condition of her body that she had first been made comatose but had regained consciousness just as her murderers were in the act of decapitating her. Included in the evidence subsequently brought forward was the fact that Walling had earlier said he needed a human head to help him with his dental studies and that after the murder Jackson had left an unevenly weighted suitcase for safe keeping with a bartender who joked that it must contain a bowling ball.

Buturlin Captain *(poisoned nineteenth century)*

As noteworthy for the death he escaped as for the death he subsequently met, the scion of a wealthy Russian family, Buturlin was poisoned by his scapegrace brother-in-law, an Irishman named O'Brien who had married the unattractive Miss Buturlin while posing as a nobleman, the Count de Lacy. The ingenious O'Brien decided that the quickest route to wealth was to inherit the money belonging to his wife's relatives, and as a first step to this end he induced Captain Buturlin to eat some slices of bread and butter that had been lavishly spread with a culture of cholera germs. Alas, the captain had been inoculated. O'Brien then encouraged him to have further inoculations; this time, he arranged for diphtheria germs to be injected into the trusting captain, who died shortly afterwards. O'Brien had been overheard instructing his medical accomplice to 'give him two phials full'.

Chesson Maria *(matricide twentieth century)*

Chesson was beaten to death by her 37-year-old son because she objected to his going for long walks and refused to buy him any more pairs of shoes.

Christofi Mrs *(murdered 1925)*

Mrs Christofi died when her daughter-in-law thrust a
burning torch down her throat and choked her to death on
the smouldering log. At the trial in Greece the
daughter-in-law, Stylou Christofi, was acquitted. Nineteen
years later, now a mother-in-law herself and living with
her son and his German wife Hella in Kentish Town,
London, Mrs Christofi the Second struck once more.
Savagely jealous of her own daughter-in-law, perhaps all
too fearful of what such a relation might want to do to *her*,
she lured her down their garden, smashed her skull with
an ashplate from the kitchen stove, then strangled her to
death. This time Mrs Christofi had her deserts. She was
hanged on 13 December 1954.

Connelly Guilym *(stabbed in error twentieth century)*

Connelly was accidentally killed by his wife while she was cutting sandwiches with a sharp knife and gesticulated too enthusiastically as he was standing nearby.

Czermak Mr *(crushed twentieth century)*

Czechoslovak Vera Czermak learnt to her distress that her husband was being unfaithful to her. It was with no more than the desire to end her miseries that she forthwith tossed herself out of her third-floor flat window in Prague. With a fine sense of irony, her leap earned her the revenge that might not have otherwise been hers. Just as she jumped, her husband walked beneath the window. She landed squarely on top of the philanderer. Vera was only injured, Mr Czermak, for his sins, was struck dead.

Ellingson Mrs *(killed by daughter 1925)*

Sixteen-year-old Dorothy Ellingson was told by her mother that on no account would she be permitted to continue her fast career through Los Angeles' raciest niteries. In reply, the girl the press christened a 'dance-mad flapper' shot her mother dead. In her defence, young Dorothy pleaded an acute case of 'Jazzmania . . . a new mental ailment'.

Guay Rita *(blown up in mid-air 1949)*

Rita Guay was married in 1949 to Albert Guay. Albert was by no means the faithful husband. So alluring was his mistress, one Marguerite Pitre, that he decided to do away with his legal spouse. Using Pitre as his dogsbody, Guay prepared a timebomb for the destruction of his wife. When she set off on a Canadian Pacific Airlines DC3, intending to visit a friend on the other side of Canada, she and the other nineteen passengers and four crew were unaware that a 2¾ lb bomb was nestling in the luggage hold. Guay had intended that the bomb explode over the sea, thus ensuring no evidence would be found. In the event, the flight took off late and the plane was still above land when the explosives, packed into a clock and secreted without her knowledge in Rita Guay's luggage, went off and blew the plane and its passengers into atoms. Guay, who had manipulated Pitre quite satisfactorily, now realised that here was his weak link; he suggested she commit suicide. Such devotion proved beyond her, but only postponed her demise. Canadian police checked the debris, and noted that one parcel, the bomb that Guay had added to his wife's luggage, was being sent to a fictitious name at a fictitious address. When the taxi driver who had driven Guay to the airport – when he was placing the bomb – identified his fare, the chase was over. Guay, Pitre and one Genereaux Ruest, a crippled watchmaker who had assembled the bomb, were all hanged for murder in 1951.

Hargis Mr *(murdered c.* 1970)

Carol Hargis hated her husband. She decided to kill him. Living in California in the hippie 1960s, she chose a suitable method: a massive dose of mind-bending LSD. This had no effect. Indeed, LSD was a bad choice since at best (worst?) it would destroy his sanity, not his body. She then turned more practical with a blackberry pie containing the venom sac of a tarantula: another failure. In quick succession came the sabotage of his truck with a home-made bomb, a live electric wire in his shower, tranquillisers in his beer and an injection of air into his veins. The method that finally earned Mrs Hargis her life term was hitting him over the head with a steel weight.

Highway Kevin *(beaten to death 1959)*

A five-month-old baby was punched to death by his father in Manchester in 1959 because his crying was interrupting a favourite television programme.

Hurley Adrian *(asphyxiated 1959)*

A six-month-old Warwick baby was accidentally asphyxiated in 1959. His father had become furious because Adrian's constant crying kept interrupting his parents as they were trying to say their prayers, so he tied a shawl around the baby's mouth to silence it sufficiently to allow the prayers to proceed in peace. The silence he achieved for his devotions was a permanent one.

James Mary *(murdered 1935)*

Mary James was the fifth wife of Los Angeles barber Robert James. Unfortunately for her there were a couple of things she didn't know about her husband. The first was that a predecessor, James's third wife, had died by drowning in her bath, leaving a convenient $20,000 insurance money for her husband. The second, and more immediate, was that shortly after their marriage Robert had contacted a friend of his, one 'Chuck' Hope, and asked him to get hold of a couple of rattlesnakes. A friend, he claimed, wanted to get rid of his wife. Hope took his commission without question. Later he was to justify this and subsequent actions by saying that Robert James, so like the snakes he admired, had hypnotised him. The offer of $100 for a 'hot' pair may have tipped the scales yet further. His early efforts to find a pair of killer snakes were fruitless. As his offerings failed to kill even the chickens and rabbits James supplied, the would-be killer grew angrier and angrier. Finally, Hope went to Pasadena and obtained two rattlers from a snake specialist, 'Snake Joe'. When they hit with deadly efficiency James was delighted.

At once he told Hope that he, not a friend, wanted the snakes and demanded his aid in disposing of his wife. Mary James, who apparently thought she was being prepared for an illicit abortion, found herself grabbed and placed, fully conscious, across the kitchen table. James used the family clothes line to tie her down and then blinded her eyes and silenced her mouth with adhesive tape. Next he placed the box of rattlesnakes on the table and forced her naked foot among the writhing creatures, which struck again and again at her defenceless flesh. Leaving her to die, the two men retired to the garage for sandwiches and a drink. When they returned to the kitchen they were surprised to find their victim still alive. James was undeterred. He loosened his wife's bonds and, helped by the 'hypnotised' Hope, dragged her weak body into the bathroom. He filled the bath with water and held her under until she finally breathed her last. It was only a letter to the police from a woman whom he subsequently jilted that led to James's arrest, trial and eventual execution.

De Kaplany Hajna *(tortured 1962)*

Hajna de Kaplany was a 25-year-old model who had recently married one Dr Geza de Kaplany, a refugee from Hungary and an anaesthetist in California's San José Hospital, The doctor, an obsessively jealous man, decided that only by disfiguring her could he ensure that his attractive young wife would be safe from the passes and temptations of other men. They had been married only five weeks when he set out to defend his bride against any possible advances. He stripped her, bound her naked body at the wrists and ankles with electric flex, covered her mouth with adhesive tape and placed in front of her eyes a scrawled message that stated, 'If you want to live do not shout, do what I tell you or you will die.' Then he donned a pair of rubber gloves, turned up the classical music on the radiogram to full blast and began applying nitric, sulphuric and hydrochloric acid to all parts of his wife's defenceless body. For all his orders not to scream, the appalling agonies that the acid was inflicting left the young woman no possibility of silence. Soon neighbours heard the screams coming from the Kaplany apartment, as the wailing sounds cut through even the noisy music. When the police smashed their way into the apartment they found Hajna hideously disfigured but still alive, her whole body savaged by third-degree burns. It took thirty-three days of unspeakable pain before Hajna de Kaplany was allowed the peace of death. Her husband was gaoled from 1963 to 1976 when he was paroled.

Kirby Emily *(buried alive twentieth century)*

Mrs Kirby was buried alive while unconscious, by her own grandson. The latter persuaded her and her second husband, Thomas Kirby, to walk with him into a field. There he knocked them both unconscious, robbed them and buried them alive in a grave he had dug. The bodies were still warm when they were found a day later.

Letgert Louisa *(murdered 1897)*

Louisa Letgert was the wife of a German sausage-maker, Adolf Letgert. Apart from his successful business recycling the otherwise unwanted portions of dead animals, Adolf Letgert fancied himself with the ladies. Poor Louisa found it increasingly hard to put up with her husband's philandering, but the day on which she decided to put her foot down and complain was the day she signed her own death warrant. First of all Adolf tried to throttle his wife in a rage, but she managed to struggle free. For a few days it seemed as if everything would return to normal. Then a truck arrived at the Letgert works. It contained 50 lb of arsenic and 325 lb of potash. Adolf claimed the chemicals were for scouring the insides of his great sausage meat vats. Then, a few days later, Louisa Letgert went missing. When friends and factory workers started inquiring as to what had happened to his wife, Adolf grew increasingly nervous and tight-lipped. One employee, more a friend of the wife than the husband, tipped off the police. They arrived and started searching the sausage factory. In a short while they knew the grim truth: in one mighty vat they found fragments of her bones and teeth. Letgert confessed, prompted by a worker who could no longer remain silent, even though his boss had offered him 'a good job for the rest of his life if he kept quiet'. Sure enough, Letgert had strangled his wife. Then he had put the arsenic, potash and the still warm corpse into a vat more accustomed to cooking animals than human meat. Then the cauldron was heated and, as the arsenic and potash ate into her flesh, Louisa Letgert, but for those incriminatory fragments, was melted into anonymity. What chunks were left at the end were dumped with usual factory waste. Adolf Letgert was executed; his death was simpler than that he gave his unfortunate spouse.

Makinson Muriel *(killed in secret 1943)*

A two-year-old North London girl mysteriously disappeared from the midst of her family of eleven brothers and sisters in 1943. Eight years later her sister Ann, then sixteen years old, was putting her brothers' football away in a sack on top of a cupboard when she found Muriel's body in the sack. Muriel's mother then admitted that she had accidentally knocked Muriel against the stove, fracturing her skull, back in 1943, and had hidden the body. The rest of the family had apparently accepted Muriel's disappearance at the time as casually as they greeted her rediscovery eight years later.

Papas Nick *(stabbed 1977)*

Forty-six-year-old Papas of Los Angeles, California, was stabbed to death after refusing to kiss his common-law wife, Mary Smith, the customary goodnight. Ms Smith used a handy butcher's knife for the assault.

Parterie Farmer *(scalded, burnt, strangled)*

Farmer Parterie was killed by his wife and stepdaughter, who poured boiling water over his head while he was asleep. This failing, they beat him with a red hot iron bar and when that was unsuccessful they finally strangled him.

Perrochet Claire *(dismembered 1973)*

Claire Perrochet wasn't even living with her husband Claude, the ex-mayor of a Swiss town, when he killed her. Despite their estrangement, Perrochet claimed he had hacked his ex-wife to pieces and disposed of her body in a nearby lake because she lived 'in intolerable disorder' and, as such, was a shame to his family.

Staunton Harriet *(starved to death 1877)*

Harriet was a naïve and foolish girl who fell easy prey to her husband, the heartless Louis Staunton. The couple lived in the small town of Penge, where Louis was busy having an affair with one Alice Rhodes. Given her simple nature, it had taken no great effort for Louis to persuade his young wife to part with such wealth as she had – roughly £3,000. But this did not satisfy him. He determined to get rid of this impediment to his pleasures. Intending to carry out 'a perfect murder', Staunton decided that enforced starvation would serve his purposes best. To this end he simply locked his wife up in October 1876 and fed her little more than bread and water for the next seven months until she died. At her death she weighed a mere 5 stone and 4 pounds. Her clothes hung in tatters from her skeletal frame and her body and hair were covered in vermin. She was discovered soon after her death. What made Staunton's efforts even more grotesque was that in an attempt to fool the inevitable coroner's court he had tried to force some morsels of chewed food down her stiffening dead throat. It was only the petition of some 700 doctors that, despite the obvious facts of the case, Harriet Staunton might by remote possibility have died of tubercular meningitis that saved Staunton, Rhodes and two of Staunton's brothers from the gallows. Instead Rhodes was set free, and the Stauntons served life terms in gaol.

Sweet Mrs *(murdered nineteenth century)*

Mrs Sweet was murdered in nineteenth-century London by her husband. The inappropriately named Mr Sweet performed the extraordinary feat of running his sword completely through her head – in one side and out the other.

Trichard M. *(shot 1978)*

Trichard, a French farmer who lived at Mexmieux, near Lyons, was watching the World Cup on television one June evening when his wife, Claudi Trichard, asked him to help pod the peas for supper. Although France had long since been dismissed from the competition, M. Trichard refused. In the argument that followed, Mme Claudi took down their shotgun from the wall, turned on her husband and blew off his head.

Death by misadventure

Anacreon *(choked sixth century BC)*

The famous Greek lyric poet was choked to death by a grape stone while drinking.

Anonymous American male *(stabbed 1969)*

A man had just picked up his wife from the café where she worked in Houston, Texas, and was driving her home. As they crossed a set of traffic lights another car ran the red light and smashed into the rear of their vehicle. It drove on a couple of blocks, when both cars pulled up. Before leaving his car the aggrieved driver put a large hunting knife into his pocket, then advanced on the man who had hit him. This driver, by now, had left his car and was moving towards the driver whom he had hit, keeping one hand in his pocket all the time. He started to swear, and the first driver asked him: 'How come you hit my car?' At this point both men revealed their knives. In the words of the aggrieved driver:

I got my knife from my pocket. The other man cut my arm, I cut him back on the face. He staggered back and started to change hands. Then the man came at me again and knocked me down and knocked the knife out of my hand. Some way or another I managed to get the knife off the ground and he came back at me and I had started getting off the ground and I stabbed him. I don't know just how many times.

As the other man staggered back to his car, the first driver returned to his own car and wife. They drove off. 'On my

way home,' after another journey, 'I drove down past the
street where the incident had occurred and I looked to see
if the car was still there. It was not. I thought that the man
was all right and I went on home.' The man was not all
right. He was dead. An unexceptional, commonplace
death, but a death none the less. The case never went to
trial on lack of evidence for a grand jury.

Anonymous bride *(killed during a game c.1820)*

Some time around 1820 a Norfolk wedding party turned
for after-dinner amusement to a game of hide and seek.
Soon it was the turn of the young bride, still dressed in her
wedding finery, to hide. She left the party and vanished.
At first, when no one could find her, the party was only
amused. Gradually, when the most intense search and
endless shouting failed to produce her, the laughter
turned to worry. But no one, including a distraught
bridegroom, could find her. In the end the party
dispersed, the bridegroom accepted his instant separation,
and life went on. It was only three years later, when by
chance the heavy lid of an old oak chest was dragged open,
that the mysterious vanishing act was explained. There, a
skeleton clad in the faded rags of a wedding dress, lay the
bride. She had climbed into the chest which closed with a
spring lock, and had been unable to get out or summon
any help. She had probably fainted, then died of starvation
and asphyxia in her wooden tomb.

Anonymous Canadian pilot *(blew himself up 1976)*

After the engine of his small plane failed, a Canadian pilot
managed to crash land in rough country. Neither the pilot
nor his fellow-flier was hurt. They decided that the
passenger should go for help, while the pilot should stay by
his plane. After a long, cold and uncomfortable night the
pilot was overjoyed as he heard the steady beat of a rescue

helicopter coming towards him. Waving a hand flare he rushed out of his plane, brandishing the flare at the helicopter and watching it come closer and closer. Leaping up and down with excitement, he tossed the flare away, still alight. Unfortunately for the pilot, while he had nursed the plane into land safely enough, the crash had ruptured his fuel tank. The fuel had seeped away all through the night. The ground all round him was deeply impregnated. As the flaming torch hit the earth the fuel ignited, and in a massive explosion the fuel, the plane and its luckless pilot were atomised, as the horrified rescuers could only stare from a mercifully safe distance.

Anonymous diver *(suffocated 1965)*

A diver was exploring the bottom of the Mediterranean using just a snorkel, which poked its snout above the waves. As he watched the flora and fauna of the sea, a bee settled on the end of his breathing apparatus. At the same instant he inhaled. The bee was sucked through the snorkel tube, down his throat, where it stung him. Trapped under water, the diver suffocated, victim of a horrible freak circumstance.

Anonymous English male *(shot 1763)*

History records the doings of John Wilkes, the eighteenth-century politician and hellraiser, but does not record the name of the man in the red waistcoat for whose death Wilkes was indirectly responsible. When Wilkes was in gaol in 1763, mobs gathered outside his cell window every day to express support for him. Finally the mob, led by a young man wearing a red waistcoat, attacked a company of soldiers who had been placed under Wilkes's window to control the crowd. After a violent struggle, the man in the red waistcoat ran away, hotly pursued by four soldiers. Their quarry turned into an alley; rounding the corner after him, they broke into an outhouse where they found a young man in a red waistcoat sitting on the latrine seat. They promptly shot him dead, only to find out that he was a respectable citizen who was genuinely relieving himself and had nothing to do with the mob attack.

Anonymous English male
(electrocuted twentieth century)

A particularly dramatic electrocution is recorded by the famous forensic pathologist Sir Francis Camps. A boy climbed up a pylon carrying electric cables across the Thames with the specific intention of throwing over the cables an arrangement of two metal cups tied together, in order to see what would happen. There was a flash of light so brilliant it was seen for miles, and the boy was hurled to the foot of the pylon, where he was found with a broken neck and widespread electrical burns down one entire side of his body, giving his flesh a 'crocodile skin' appearance.

Anonymous English male *(swallowed molten metal)*

A case recorded by Gould and Pyle *(see* bibliography) is that of the man who was looking upwards at the Eddystone lighthouse fire, with his mouth open, when he was killed by a mass of molten lead falling on to his face and into his mouth. Over 200 grams of lead were found in his stomach after death.

Anonymous German glider pilots
(frozen to death 1935)

As five pilots flew their gliders over the Rhine Valley in Germany they found themselves suddenly caught in the convectional updraughts of a huge storm cloud. Fearing their gliders would be shaken to pieces they all baled out and assumed their parachutes would take them safely to earth. They were tragically mistaken. Almost at once they were thrown several hundred feet vertically upwards. As the updraught lessened they began to fall – until once again they were tossed upwards by a new updraught. Over and over the process repeated until finally the five reached the ground. Caught for hours in the freezing temperatures, only one survived. The other four arrived on earth frozen to death as human hailstones.

Anonymous sailors *(drowned 1970)*

Four amateurs were sailing in a 35 foot motor boat. Two of them were experienced, two merely passengers. The wind was brisk, force 5 or 6, but no one had bothered with a life jacket. Suddenly the boat gybed just as the mate stood up. Stunned, he fell over the side. The captain, the other experienced sailor, faced an agonising decision: if he went over the side for his friend, could the passengers help? He brought the boat back to the mate, leapt overboard and grabbed hold of him. He shouted to the others to throw him a loop of rope to help him and the stunned mate back on board. But the passengers were frightened and incapable. They watched, powerless and terrified, as both the captain and the mate slipped beneath the waves.

Anonymous US Army deserters
(roasted alive 1979)

Two young men, perhaps US Army deserters trying to get
back home from Europe, sealed themselves into a
container of paper which was being shipped from Finland
to California. When the package was finally opened at an
office of the Pacific Press Company at Vernon, California,
it seemed to witnesses as if the duo had been 'cooked alive'.
Their month-long journey left them trapped in
temperatures of 150° to 160° Farenheit – first in the hold
of a ship, and then on the long journey across the broiling
deserts of the US South West.

Anonymous air crash victims *(1970)*

Eleven people were killed on 8 September 1970 at JFK
Airport in New York when a $10 million DC-8 aircraft was
destroyed by a pebble. The plane crashed on take-off.
Subsequent investigation revealed that, as it was taxiing
into position, the blast of its engines had hurled a small
asphalt-covered pebble into the air, which had landed
right on top of the plane's tail – in itself improbable – and
from there had rolled down to lodge between the
horizontal stabiliser and the elevator. When the pilot
applied up-elevator pressure on his controls, the pebble
had jammed them in this position and the plane had
consequently stalled and crashed.

Bonham A. V. *(shot by his own gun 1928)*

Mr Bonham, of Cotter, Arkansas, came home to see smoke
billowing from his own home. It seemed that his
twelve-year-old son had been playing around with petrol
and matches and in the resulting explosion had set his
father's house on fire. With commendable calm, Bonham
recruited various helpers and started removing what he

could from the burning house. Nearly everything was out and Bonham was watching sadly as the flames ate into his home when there was a sudden report. Mack Medley, a neighbour, felt something brush the peak of his cap, and saw Bonham collapse to the ground, shouting, 'I'm shot!' Then he staggered a few steps and fell again, quite dead. Alas, Mr Bonham's careful house clearance had overlooked one vital possession – a loaded revolver which he kept in a bureau drawer. The flames had reached the bureau and their heat set off the gun. It was Bonham's terrible misfortune to be standing directly in the line of fire when the stray bullet set out.

Chrysippus *(died laughing third century BC)*

Chrysippus, a Greek philosopher, is said to have died of laughter when he found the sight of a donkey eating figs more than his sense of humour could take.

Collyer Langley *(crushed by debris 1947)*

Langley Collyer and his brother Homer were ageing recluses who lived together in an apartment of rooms and rooms filled with debris. For fear of burglars, Langley, the healthier of the two, erected careful booby traps around the cluttered house. Unfortunately, as he carried a tray of food to his ailing brother, Langley triggered off one of the traps himself and died submerged beneath a pile of old newspapers, three breadboxes, a sewing machine and a suitcase filled with heavy scrap metal. Homer, bereft of food, starved to death. It took police three weeks before they unearthed the bodies.

Crokhay Gertrude *(died of shock sixteenth century)*

According to Foxe's *Book Of Martyrs*, this good woman of the sixteenth century died of an illness brought on by shock when, while wrongfully imprisoned in Antwerp, she saw other prisoners being drowned in Rhenish wine vats and cast into the river in sacks.

Feller Joachim
(sleepwalked to death seventeenth century)

A seventeenth century German poet was killed when he walked straight out of an upstairs window during a bout of somnambulism.

Foard Raymond R. *(fell to death 1977)*

On returning to his apartment building in Maryland one evening in 1977, Foard discovered that he had forgotten his keys and was locked out. Rather than waste time calling help, Foard decided to climb up the side of his building, aiming for the seventh floor on which his flat was situated. He had just pulled himself laboriously as far as the fifth floor when a woman, sitting on her balcony, heard heavy breathing and saw a hand grasp the edge of the balcony. She screamed with shock, Foard lost his concentration and – tragically – his grip and plunged down to die on the concrete below.

Fulk Fitzwarine IV *(suffocated 1264)*

This English baron of the thirteenth century suffocated within his own armour, aged thirty-four, when his horse became caught fast in a bog after the Battle of Lewes.

Grant Betty and Malins June
(poisoned twentieth century)

They were killed by an aphrodisiac administered without their knowledge by an amorous workmate. One of their fellow-workers in a firm of wholesale chemists gave Betty Grant a single piece of chocolate-covered coconut ice, into which he had inserted some cantharidin, a key component of the traditional aphrodisiac Spanish fly. Unknown to the would-be lover, cantharidin is a deadly poison, even in minute quantities, and when Betty Grant shared her single piece of coconut ice with June Malins, both girls were irretrievably doomed. They died within twenty-four hours.

Green Charlie *(froze to death twentieth century)*

This black trombone player froze to death while sleeping on his doorstep, having found himself locked out of his New York house on a February night in 1936.

Hallam-Radcliffe Basil
(strangled by a parachute c.1915)

There was nothing funny about the manner of Hallam-Radcliffe's (otherwise known as comedian Basil Hallam, or 'Gilbert the Filbert, Kernel of the Nuts') demise. He was aloft at 10,000 feet in an observation balloon spotting enemy gun positions when something cut through the balloon's retaining wire and set it adrift. He put on his parachute and jumped, but the parachute became caught in the basket of the balloon. As his friends watched helplessly, he was slowly strangled by its ropes as he descended.

Huskisson William *(first railway victim 1830)*

This English politician died from injuries caused when he was run over by a steam train, Stephenson's pioneering *Rocket*, at the official opening of the Liverpool–Manchester railway line in 1830. A statue of Huskisson, dressed in a Roman toga, commemorates him in Pimlico Gardens, London.

John Brynmor *(electrocuted 1926)*

A young Welsh coal miner was electrocuted in freakishly unlucky circumstances in 1926 by an electrified security fence around a coal yard. The fence carried too low a voltage to be dangerous under normal conditions, but it was raining at the time and John was running away from something that had frightened him. In his already alarmed state, he slipped and put out his wet hand to grasp the wet wire of the electrified fence, at the same time as the other hand, also wet, contacted a wet sheet of corrugated zinc that happened to by lying beside the fence.

Killian William *(shot by a duffle bag 1976)*

William Killian, an employee of Frontier Airlines in Denver, Colorado, was moving a passenger's baggage. When he picked up a duffle bag the revolver which this bag contained went off. It fired a bullet into the baggage handler, killing him at once. No charges were ever filed.

Laroya Wesley and Helen *(died in a hot tub 1979)*

Age is no bar for fun-loving couples in California. Fifty-eight-year-old retired naval lieutenant-commander Wesley Laroya and his 53-year-old wife Helen had succumbed happily to the hot tub craze and had one installed in the backyard of their home in Simi Valley. Both Laroyas suffered from dangerously high blood pressure, but this never deterred them from their fun and games. One night in May 1979 the pair slipped into the hot tub, turned up the thermostat to 110° Fahrenheit and fell asleep. They never awoke. Police investigations showed that both had been drinking heavily and the heat of the tub, their own blood pressure and the alcohol had combined to cause deaths attributed to hyperthermia, ethylism (alcohol poisoning) and heart disease.

Laslett Jane *(eaten by rats nineteenth century)*

Jane was the thirteen-year-old daughter of Mr and Mrs William Laslett, of the town of Haverball, in nineteenth-century England. Laslett was a travelling salesman, and on one of his trips away from home he took his wife and left young Jane behind to look after the house. The neighbours saw her around the house for a day or so, and then after a further few days realised that she seemed to have disappeared. Because the house was locked they assumed she had gone to join her parents. Finally an increasing odour of decay led them to have the house broken into. They found Jane's body in the basement, covered in rats that had already devoured most of it.

Lee David *(beheaded by accident twentieth century)*

A Canadian scientist, Lee had his head chopped off by a helicopter when he failed to bend down as he walked under the whirring rotor blades. To add insult to injury, a Quebec court of appeal subsequently ruled that his estate would have to pay for the damage done to the helicopter.

Little William *(lynched 1919)*

A black soldier returning from the First World War to Blakely, Georgia, in 1919 was beaten to death by a mob of local whites when he got off the train because he refused to obey their order to take off his army uniform and walk home in his underwear.

Lully Raymond *(stoned to death)*

This medieval philosopher invented a logical machine with which he hoped to demonstrate the nature of truth. He was stoned to death for his pains.

Martin Carroll *(impaled c.1930)*

Martin was killed by an extremely unlikely instrument of death. He played trombone with Isham Jones's orchestra in Chicago. He was travelling to an engagement in a car that suddenly braked, throwing him forward on to the trombone with such force that it pierced his heart and lungs.

Merrick John *(the 'Elephant Man' died in bed 1890)*

Perhaps the saddest of all deaths recorded in these pages: Merrick was the terribly disfigured natural freak known as the 'Elephant Man' who was exhibited by showmen in late nineteenth-century London and then mercifully confined to a hospital ward for the rest of his life. His body was covered by tumours caused by neurofibromatosis. His head was so huge and heavy that he had difficulty holding it up, and he was obliged to sleep sitting up in bed with his head resting on his bent knees. One night in April 1890, he did something he had always longed to do; he slept in the normal fashion, with his head resting on a pillow. During the night, its weight dislocated his neck and killed him.

Mytton John *(died of burns 1834)*

Squire Mytton, of Halston near Shrewsbury, stands among the great British eccentrics. Completely regardless of life and limb, starting with his own and going on from there, he consumed eight bottles of port (after a while he changed it for brandy) every day, seemed to possess no fear of heat or cold, hunted, rode and drove his carriages like a man possessed, and was known to ride into dinner, dressed in hunting pink, bestride a bear, toss handfuls of banknotes rolled into lumps at whosoever might catch them. He had 152 pairs of trousers and a similar number of waistcoats, and coats, while in his cellar 'hogsheads of ale stood like soldiers in close formation'. The squire's final great excess, which led inexorably to his miserable death, came when in 1834 he became afflicted with a hiccup that would not go away. At the time Mytton was in Calais, where he had fled, since his profligacy was starting to catch up with him, as it did with many gentlemen of his era and financial straits. After, no doubt, his usual massive intake of brandy, fortified quite probably by some French wines, Mytton was still hiccupping without relief. 'Damn this hiccup,' he announced, 'I'll frighten it away.' Seizing a lighted candle, he applied it to the hem of his nightshirt and, since it was thin and cotton, it caught fire very quickly. Two friends, seeing what Mytton had done, threw themselves on him in an attempt to douse the flames, and tore the nightdress off him to make sure. 'The hiccup is gone, by God,' said Mytton. He ignored his hideous burns as, delighted by his success, he fell drunkenly between the sheets. The next morning, nothing daunted, he greeted his saviours with a loud 'View-halloo!', straight off to the hunting field, to show how well he could stand pain. But the damage was done. The burns were terrible and Mytton had to wait in Calais to recover. Then, perhaps in a foolish fit of bravado, he returned to England. His creditors gathered round and he was packed off to the King's Bench Prison. He left gaol but did not survive. The aftermath of his dreadful injuries, the rigours of prison and the wretchedness of a life in which money, friends, a once-loved wife and quite possibly his sanity as well had all departed proved all too much for an eccentric but never wicked man to bear.

O'Brien Michael *(beaten to death 1959)*

O'Brien died when he was beaten to death in mistake for someone else. His killer, a West Indian named Kelly, had been fighting with another man in an English pub. Twice Kelly was ejected from the pub, then his opponent left. Twenty minutes later, Kelly burst into the bar with a length of iron in his hand, made straight for O'Brien, who happened to be standing there with his back to Kelly, and hit him four times on the head, killing him. O'Brien had nothing to do with the fight, but was mistaken by Kelly for his opponent.

O'Malley Joseph Patrick
(electrocuted twentieth century)

O'Malley was electrocuted when he went walking beside the track of a New York subway railway line while intoxicated, and stopped to urinate. The stream of urine struck the electrified third rail and acted as a pathway for 600 volts to enter his body. The cause of his death became apparent at autopsy only when electrical burns were found on the tip of his penis and on his thumb and forefinger.

Otway Thomas *(choked 1685)*

This seventeenth-century dramatist died in destitution at the age of thirty-three. The immediate cause of his death was a loaf of bread that a well-meaning acquaintance had given him in response to his desperate begging for aid. In his starving condition he gulped the first mouthful ravenously and choked to death on it.

Payne Sharon *(shot by accident twentieth century)*

Sharon Payne was trying to cheer up a depressed friend, David Falconrie of Los Angeles, when without any warning he produced a pistol, put it to his head and pulled the trigger. Ms Payne sat appalled as the bullet killed her friend, passed through his head, ricocheted off a water-head and embedded itself right between her eyes, killing her instantly.

Phillips Charles *(fainted to death 1977)*

So excited was 31-year-old electrician Phillips on seeing his newborn son that he fainted clean away. Unfortunately in collapsing he so injured his head that he never regained consciousness and died.

Pinkerton Allan *(died of gangrene 1884)*

The founder of the famous American private detective agency died, aged sixty-five, of gangrene of the tongue after having stumbled and bitten it during a morning stroll.

Pitcairn William *(killed for a joke nineteenth century)*

A wretched tramp in nineteenth-century Staffordshire was accidentally killed by pranksters. The latter treated him to several pints of ale and, while he was half stupefied from this unwonted treat, put him into the local stocks, with his feet firmly fixed so that he could not release himself. In the morning he was found dead from malnutrition and exposure.

Rappe Virginia *(died of internal bleeding 1921)*

Virginia Rappe was a former Chicago model, once featured on the cover of the sheet-music for the hit 'Let Me Call You Sweetheart', who arrived in Hollywood, like so many others, to make it in the movies. Unlike those others, Rappe started to find parts. First as a Mack Sennett Girl, then in small roles. She won a Best Dressed Girl in Pictures award and might have justifiably felt that things were on the up. On 5 September 1921 Rappe was invited to a party in Suite 1221 of San Francisco's St Francis Hotel, hosted by gargantuan comedian Roscoe 'Fatty' Arbuckle. As the wild party went from excess to excess, Arbuckle picked up Virginia and vanished with her into one of the suite's bedrooms, remarking happily to the crowd, 'This is the chance I've been waiting for.' The door slammed behind them. Soon afterwards terrible moans and shrieks cut through the party hubbub. Inside the bedroom, when witnesses burst in, Virginia Rappe was lying, her clothes torn to shreds, screaming, 'I'm dying, he hurt me!' The comedian merely told his friends, 'Get her out of here.' Rushed to hospital suffering from a severe internal haemorrhage, Virginia Rappe died, aged just twenty-five, five days later. Whether it was the great weight of the comedian that had hurt her or, as more lurid speculation had it, his bizarre experiments with the neck of a champagne bottle was never really proved. On Rappe's death Arbuckle was charged with her murder. He was acquitted by a majority ten-to-two verdict, but the movie industry blacklisted the one-time star. He worked thenceforth only under the pseudonym William Goodrich and that only as a director. As sure as Virginia Rappe's career died in that sordid bedroom, so did that of Hollywood's briefly-favoured fat man.

Rose Thomas *(crushed by bells 1905)*

Thomas Rose, for twenty years the bellringer at Stoke-on-Trent parish church, climbed as he did every Saturday up the winding staircase to the belfry, in order to check the bells for the next morning's service. Two of his eight children waited downstairs in the church. When the children had waited longer than usual they went to fetch their mother. She too climbed the spiral stairs only to find her husband dead, crushed horribly between a giant bell and a nearby beam.

Taylor Henry *(killed by a coffin twentieth century)*

This 66-year-old man was one of the pallbearers at a funeral at Kensal Green Cemetery in London. As the coffin, which was lined with lead, was being carried down a narrow path towards the open grave, the bearers stopped to turn it around so that it could proceed head-first. In the act of so doing, Taylor stumbled and fell, and the other bearers were forced to let go of their heavy burden. The coffin fell on Taylor's head and chest, fatally injuring him.

Thirkettle Harold *(stabbed 1961)*

Himself a convicted murderer, Thirkettle is understood, from unofficial sources, to have been stabbed to death in 1961 in Dartmoor prison, more or less by accident. During a prison movie evening, a man sitting in front of Thirkettle was stabbed in the back by an assailant who then succeeded in escaping in the ensuing confusion. The stabbed man, seriously wounded, pulled the knife from his own back and in a frenzy of retaliation slashed at the two men nearest to him, one of whom was Thirkettle.

Todd Thomas *(strangled eighteenth century)*

Todd was strangled by accident when he was placed in the pillory for a minor offence in eighteenth-century England. His legs were too short to reach the ground, so he hung from the pillory with his head through the hole instead of simply standing on his feet. By the time the officials realised their mistake, it was too late.

Vance George *(accidental death nineteenth century)*

A celebrated nineteenth-century physician was accidentally killed by the impulsiveness of one of his patients. When he called upon a Mr Broadley, whom he was treating for overexcitability, the patient suddenly rushed forward to greet him as he reached the top of a staircase. So unexpected and uncontrolled was Broadley's dash forward that he collided violently with Dr Vance and sent him tumbling fatally downstairs.

Wallace George *(heart attack 1977)*

George Wallace, a 72-year-old retired chef, was a regular client at one of Auckland's massage parlours where pretty young masseuses called him Old Wally and helped him while away his dotage. Soon 'Wally' had a favourite, a seventeen-year-old amateur, who was working her way through one of New Zealand's most exclusive women's colleges on her wages from the parlour. Unfortunately for both rubber and rubbed, one afternoon in February 1977 the whole experience proved too much for the old man. As his fortnightly session came to its climax, 'Wally' sat up on the table, screamed out loud, then fell back, quite dead.

Welch Mr *(broke his spine 1904)*

Mr Welch, thirty-three, a wine dealer, returned home one night only to stumble over the coping of his front steps and collapse on the ground. When his wife, who had expected him back at seven o'clock, finally looked out of her front door three hours later, she found her husband lying paralysed and in great pain. He had been there, he explained, unable to move or cry out for some two hours. Mr Welch never recovered, dying in hospital as a result of the dislocation and fracture of his spine.

Zimmermann The Julich Giant
(suffocated c.1660)

Zimmermann was a carpenter in the Prussian town of Julich in the time of King Frederick William I. The latter prided himself on the height of his soldiers, seeking out tall recruits from far and near. His Potsdam palace was guarded by 2,400 giant grenadiers, the tallest of whom were over two metres in height. Many of these had been press-ganged into service by unscrupulous recruiting agents. One of these agents came across Zimmermann, who was almost two metres tall, and ordered from him a wooden crate just over that length. When the box was finished by the lanky carpenter, the recruiting agent provocatively declared that it was too short; so to prove that it was not, Zimmermann stepped inside it. Instantly the lid was slammed shut and the crate locked and handed over to a group of grenadiers to transport back to their headquarters. Unfortunately, the agent had omitted to include any air holes in the specifications for the crate, and Zimmermann suffocated *en route*.

Zola Emile *(asphyxiated 1902)*

The great French novelist died in 1902 of carbon monoxide poisoning, caused by the fumes from his heater which could not escape through a chimney blocked with debris.

You've got to laugh...

Alee Johnny *(heart attack 1887)*

Alee was a famous American fat man, alleged to have weighed half a ton, who died in 1887 when his weight caused him to fall through the floor of his log cabin, where he hung helplessly suspended. The actual cause of death was a heart attack brought on by the accident.

Anastasi Araldo *(killed by falling dog 1954)*

Pensioner Araldo Anastasi died in the Via dello Scalo, Rome, when a terrier called Leo, which was waiting on a fourth-floor window for his master to return, fell from the ledge and landed squarely on the hapless senior citizen's head.

Anonymous Indians *(suffocated twentieth century)*

Seven men died of suffocation near Ahmedabad in western India when one of them accidentally fell into a pit full of cow manure and the other six jumped in to rescue him.

Anonymous Italian family *(drowned in wine 1977)*

A family of four died after inhaling the fumes from a vat of fermenting wine near their home in Verona, Italy. The youngest, a boy aged seven, accidentally kicked a football into the vat. He jumped in after it and soon succumbed to

the fumes. He was followed to his death by his 51-year-old
father, his forty-year-old mother and an aunt aged
forty-four. None of them was able to escape the
overpowering strength of the wine.

Anonymous Polish immigrant *(choked 1973)*

A Polish immigrant, resident in Stoke-on-Trent for more
than twenty-five years, was unable to rid himself of a
foolish fear of vampires. Like any film-buff, he knew that
the best defence against vampires, short of a stake through
the heart, is plenty of garlic. For many years he made a
practice of sleeping with a clove of garlic in his mouth. The
vampires duly kept away, but coughing in his sleep one
night, the poor man dislodged his garlic and choked to
death on the prophylactic lump.

Aretino, Pietro *(laughed to death 1556)*

Pietro Aretino, 'one of the wittiest knaves God ever made',
was an Italian poet and playwright who delighted and
scandalised his contemporaries with his pointed, satirical
and often bawdy comedies. Aged sixty-four, he died
suitably when, convulsed with laughter at some lewd joke,
he collapsed with an apoplectic fit. As the priest smeared
his forehead with holy oil before his last breath, Aretino
told his friends: 'Keep the rats away now I'm all greased
up.'

Baxter Charles *(heart attack twentieth century)*

Charles Baxter shook hands with the Queen Mother at
Walmer in Kent and immediately collapsed from a heart
attack and died at her feet.

Britton Thomas *(frightened to death 1714)*

A dealer in coal was frightened to death in 1714 by a prank played upon him by a ventriloquist. The latter convinced Britton that a demon was speaking to him from inside his coal sack.

Bungan Sammy *(electrocuted twentieth century)*

A coroner's court in Darwin, Australia, found that Bungan had been accidentally electrocuted as a result of urinating against a live power pole.

Capello Bianca *(poisoned in error sixteenth century)*

This noblewoman of sixteenth-century Florence died when she attempted to poison the canny Cardinal Ferdinand with a specially prepared tart. The cardinal exchanged his tart for hers when she was not watching.

Caxboeck Adolph *(choked twentieth century)*

Twenty-three-year-old Caxboeck was taking part in a competition to see who could blow a ping-pong ball the farthest when he inhaled with such force that the ball was sucked down his throat and choked him.

Cook Paul Maldwyn
(accidental suicide twentieth century)

A storeman and packer of Merrylands in Sydney, Australia, this 21-year-old man died accidentally as a result of injecting himself with Vegemite (an Australian yeast extract spread, similar to Marmite).

Creekmore Woodrow W. *(crushed to death 1976)*

Woodrow W. Creekmore was driving near his hometown of Chickasha, Oklahoma, in 1976, when a tie rod on his car broke, sending the vehicle careering into a telephone pole. Fortunately for Creekmore, he walked away from the crash. Less fortunately, as he stood near his car discussing the crash with a highway patrolman, the pole in question fell over, hitting Creekmore on the head and killing him.

Danvers Edward
(collapsed in the street eighteenth century)

The death of this eighteenth-century Londoner may well have been caused by the passion of the young bloods of the day for gambling. Danvers collapsed in the street while passing Brooks, the coffee shop much patronised by men of fashion. Immediately, the young clients of Brooks began to gamble on whether or not Danvers would live or die. When others tried to help him, they were prevented from doing so on the grounds that it would affect the odds. He died.

Drummond Jack *(shot 1978)*

American mystery writer Jack Drummond, aged fifty-five, was trying to bolster his faltering career when he decided that his researches into a new book, *Bank Robber*, needed some on-the-spot, in-depth investigation. He sent a manuscript of the book to his daughter. In it he warned that his plans for research might well bring him trouble. He armed himself with a pistol and set out to rob a bank himself. Drummond was hardly able to produce the gun and threaten a bank teller when a security guard opened fire and shot him dead on the spot.

Fabius *(choked)*

A Roman praetor, Fabius was choked by a single goat hair in the milk he was drinking.

Ferrari Severiano *(heart attack 1905)*

When confined to a mental hospital in 1905, Italian poet Severiano Ferrari was informed that his fortunes had changed: he had been appointed Professor of Literature at the University of Bologna. So shocked was he by this sudden announcement that he dropped dead of a heart attack.

Fitzherbert Mrs *(died in hysterics 1782)*

Mrs Fitzherbert, a Northamptonshire widow, went on a Wednesday evening in April 1782 to see *The Beggar's Opera* a the Drury Lane Theatre. When the popular actor Mr Bannister made his first appearance dressed as Polly Peachum, the entire audience was convulsed with hilarious laughter. Some more than others: Mrs Fitzherbert was so delighted by the spectacle that she had to leave the theatre, so consuming were her cries of glee. As was reported in the *Gentleman's Magazine* a week later: 'Not being able to banish the figure from her memory, she was thrown into hysterics, which continued without intermission until she expired Friday morning.'

Flynn Private Harry *(killed 1917)*

Flynn holds the dubious distinction of being America's first casualty in the First World War. It was not a distinguished death. Flynn was by trade a fireman, attached to New York City's No. 7 hook and ladder company. Conscripted into the US Army, he started basic training in Camp Upton, Yaphank, Long Island. Flynn would never see Europe, since he died, of indigestion, before he had even completed his training, or indeed even received uniform, boots or a rifle, none of which essential kit was yet available to American troops. Despite all this, Flynn was buried with full military honours and bugles were blown ceremoniously over his coffin as it lay at his home in the Bronx. As is traditional, the Stars and Stripes were presented to the nearest relative, his uncle Tom.

Gallus *(heart attack?)*

This Roman praetor died while kissing the hand of his wife.

Harkan Peter *(pulled to death nineteenth century)*

Harkan was a demonstrator for Phillip Crampton, surgeon at Meath Hospital in the early years of the nineteenth century and director of a school of anatomy that made use of bodies supplied by grave-robbers. Harkan died of internal injuries received during a midnight body-snatching escapade in a cemetery, when he was the subject of a tug-of-war between a group of students and a watchman. The latter grabbed him by the legs as he was climbing over the cemetery wall; the students took his arms from the other side to help him escape and both sides pulled heartily.

Krios Argyrios *(killed by a cow 1977)*

Krios was killed in December 1977 when the family cow, which he was attempting to slaughter for the Christmas festivities, turned nasty and killed him instead.

Lenfant *(killed by a billiard ball 1843)*

Lenfant was killed in a duel with a gentleman named Mellant in France. The oddity about the duel was that it was fought with billiard balls, or rather with a single red billiard ball. The two had quarrelled over a game of billiards and drew lots to see who would have first go at hurling the ball at the other. Mellant won and threw the ball hard and straight, hitting Lenfant on the forehead, killing him instantly.

Lepidus *(died of shock)*

Lepidus died from the shock of stubbing his big toe on a doorstep.

Li Po *(drowned 762)*

Li Po was both a great Chinese poet and great drunkard, and the fantasies of the first attainment combined with those of the second led to his death. His admirer, the Emperor Ming Huang, did him the singular honour of acting as his secretary and slavishly jotted down every mellifluous line. He also indulged Li Po's endless thirst by giving him a pension that included the right to free drinks at every inn. One night, well drunk, Li Po decided to sail on a river. Seeing the reflection of the moon on the water and wondering at its poetic charms, he tried to kiss it. Alas, the romantic lust for lunar communication was not helped by his drunken inability to keep his balance. The great poet slipped, fell in and was lost beneath the waters for ever.

Llegas Al *(killed by fighting cock 1970)*

Fifty-nine-year-old Llegas trained fighting cocks for illegal contests. Armed with lethal razor-sharp gaffs, the cocks fought to the death for high-stakes punters. Llegas died when he bled to death after one of his own birds turned on him. Said a friend: 'I saw the chicken stab him twice, quick, quick.' Two years later a cockfight referee in the Philippines must have said something one of the birds resented, since during a fight at a Manila cockpit he was so badly attacked by one of the lethally armed birds that he died of his wounds.

Lully Jean-Baptiste
(blood poisoning seventeenth century)

This seventeeth-century French composer died as a result of hitting himself on the big toe while conducting one of his own works, a *Te Deum* that was being performed to celebrate the king's recovery from a serious illness. In those days, conductors indicated the rhythm by hitting the ground with a long, heavy baton. Lully hit his toe instead of the ground on one of his downward strokes and the fatal blood poisoning set in.

Margutte *(died of laughter)*

Margutte died laughing while watching a monkey trying to pull on a pair of boots.

Maldi Sebastiano *(blown up 1819)*

This Italian opera singer came to London early in the nineteenth century and made a name for himself in *buffo* roles. He was killed in Paris in 1819 when a pressure cooker, which had just been invented, exploded as he was standing nearby.

Marsh Cyrus *(drowned nineteenth century)*

A travelling showman in late-nineteenth-century Indiana, Marsh went from town to town pulling his cart behind him and attracting considerable attention in the process with his amusing impression of a horse. No doubt in the attempt to add even greater verisimilitude to his horse act, he shied at a piece of paper one day while crossing a bridge, could not recover his balance, fell into the creek below with his cart and was drowned.

Miller Gary *(burnt to death 1976)*

Fireman Gary Miller was victim of a horrible double irony when he died in November 1976. Miller, of St Joseph, Missouri, was asleep and off duty when a fire broke out in his home and killed him. An uninstalled smoke detector was found among the debris, still in its package. It was still dutifully ringing.

Mitchell Alex *(laughed to death 1975)*

Fifty-year-old Mitchell, a bricklayer of Kings Lynn, Norfolk, was happily enjoying his favourite TV comedy show, *The Goodies*, alongside his wife Nessie. When the

comedy trio reached a sketch about a spoof Kung Fu from
Lancashire called 'Ecky Thump', Mr Mitchell couldn't stop
laughing. After half an hour of absolute hysteria he
suffered a heart attack and died. His wife wrote later to the
Goodies and thanked them for making her late husband's
last thirty minutes so incomparably happy.

Philemon *(laughed to death 263? BC)*

Philemon, a writer of comedies, apparently found one of
his own jokes so enthralling that he was unable to recover
from the fit of laughter that such ribaldry induced. It is
unknown whether this fatal self-congratulation led to the
general sneering at those who laugh at their own jokes.

Pique Monsieur de *(lost a duel in balloons 1808)*

M. de Pique was the loser of an unusual duel in
early-nineteenth-century Paris. His opponent was
Monsieur de Grandpré, the cause of the duel was a dispute
over Mlle Tirevit, a famous *danseuse* and the weapons
chosen were balloons and blunderbusses. Each man went
aloft on 3 May 1808 in a separate balloon near the
Tuileries, with a crowd of interested spectators watching.
At a height of 610 metres, they discharged their
blunderbusses at each other's balloon. M. de Pique missed
but his opponent did not. De Pique's balloon was
punctured so severely it crashed straight to the ground,
killing him on impact.

Priestley Raymond *(brain damage twentieth century)*

Raymond Priestley, of Melbourne, Australia, was playing
snooker in his garage with a friend. So enthusiastic did he
become that he attempted a highly acrobatic trick shot. He
climbed on to a crossbeam, hung upside down with his
weight supported by his legs and prepared to cue his shot.

He slipped, falling head-first on to the concrete garage floor before he could address the ball. The injuries he received on hitting the floor were sufficient to kill him from brain damage.

Quinquandon Marc *(indigestion twentieth century)*

The world snail-eating champion, 27-year-old Quinquandon died of indigestion in Nancy, France, after collapsing during a snail-eating exhibition. He had just eaten 72 snails in three minutes at a village dance. A bulldozer driver, he had become world champion four months earlier by eating 144 snails in eleven and a half minutes.

Riegger Wallingford *(tripped over doglead)*

This twentieth-century American composer shared the manner of his demise with the last of the Bonapartes; he tripped over a doglead. Cat-fanciers need not congratulate themselves – there's always toxoplasmosis. Bird-lovers risk psittacosis. And Bradley J. Baxter, of Wichita, Kansas, was strangled in his sleep by his pet orang-utan.

Shoesmith Christopher *(burned to death)*

Sixty-year-old proprietor of the Royal Midshipman tavern of Clerkenwell, Shoesmith was burned to death by his own whisky. He was tapping a large barrel in the cellar when the tap broke, the bung came loose and whisky shot out under pressure all over the cellar. At this inauspicious moment Shoesmith made the fatal mistake of calling for a lighted candle so that he could see more clearly.

Shortis William and Emily Ann *(crushed 1903)*

Mr and Mrs Shortis, both around seventy years old, lived together at Oakes Street, Liverpool. Neither had been seen for several days in August 1903, and neighbours summoned the police. When the constables entered, they found William lying prone at the foot of the stairs, only barely alive, and sixteen-stone Emily already dead, pinning his much thinner body to the floor. It was deduced that the two had been going upstairs, William behind his wife, when Emily tripped and fell back, crushing her husband in her fall and dying at once from injuries she received in the fall. William Shortis remained thus pinioned for three days before he was discovered.

Steininger Hans *(tripped to death 1567)*

Austrian burgher Hans Steininger claimed and was respected for possessing the longest beard in the world. One day, in September 1567, Hans was climbing the steps that lead to the council chamber in the town of Brunn. As he made his way upwards, he stepped on his beard, tripped over and tumbled down the flight of stone stairs. He died of the head injuries he received as he fell.

Stobb *(exploded self twentieth century)*

Ripley's *Believe It Or Not!* recounts the tale of a Russian workman, one Stobb, who managed to bring truth to that popular fantasy of breath so overloaded with alcohol that you could light it. After drinking an enormous quantity of vodka, Stobb decided to smoke a cigarette. It was when he attempted to blow out his match that he made his mistake. Flames shot from his mouth and an explosion followed. Stobb collapsed to the floor, severely injured and unconscious. He died shortly after.

Tice Reuben *(killed by own invention 1967)*

Reuben Tice, an electrician of Monterey, California, devoted his real enthusiasms to his career as an amateur inventor. He had achieved some success with his ideas for under-floor heating as well as a device for chilling cocktail glasses. In November 1967, aged sixty-eight, Tice embarked on his masterwork: a device for taking the wrinkles out of prunes. The need for such an invention is unclear, but all was going well enough at first. Then, tragically, the fledgling machine exploded, and a ten-inch-long steel cylinder struck Tice on the head. His dead body was discovered stretched across his workbench, surrounded by the shattered machine and half a pound of prunes. Alas, they were still wrinkled.

Todd Captain Valentine *(shot dead 1899)*

A much-quoted case of cadaveric spasm or instantaneous *rigor mortis*. During the siege of Ladysmith in the Boer War, while some of the defending British soldiers were playing cricket, a shell from the besieging artillery killed Captain Todd while he was in the act of bowling. His death was instantaneous, and the ball remained firmly clutched in his lifeless hand. After some debate between the umpires, the ball was declared dead.

Toivio Pastor Kaarlo
(electrocuted twentieth century)

This 62-year-old Swedish clergyman was electrocuted while baptising new church members. He was standing in a heated pool preparing for the ceremony when an assistant handed him a live microphone.

Toward Mary *(killed 1959)*

The murder of Mary Toward in 1959 is of interest not so much for its manner (straightforward strangling) as for the manner in which its perpetrator, her husband John, unsuccessfully attempted suicide in a fit of remorse. He climbed on top of a high wall overlooking a dock and proceeded to drink a bottle of whisky in the hope that he would fall asleep on his precarious perch and fall off, killing himself. He did indeed fall off, but found himself simply hanging upside down with his feet entangled in some electric cables – where he remained until he was rescued to stand trial.

Vickers Wayne *(crushed twentieth century)*

Vickers was a textile worker of Rutherford County who was wound into the middle of a huge roll of cloth. His body was not found until the roll was finally unwound.

Walker Maude *(heart attack twentieth century)*

Mrs Walker, a 59-year-old TV quiz contestant, had just succeeded in winning her round of the show *Temptation*. She barely had time to start celebrating when the emotion of the moment took over and she died on camera, struck down by a heart attack.

Whitson John *(killed by accident 1629)*

After living an adventurous life and surviving to the age of seventy-two – quite an achievement in the seventeeth century – Whitson was killed in a freak accident. He fell off his horse head-first on to a nail that happened to be standing upright on the ground outside a blacksmith's shop. The nail pierced his skull and entered the brain, causing his death.

Winikus Henry *(accidental death 1956)*

Harry Winikus loved a good practical joke. There was
nothing too bizarre for his fancy, just so long as it made
him laugh at the same time as turning everyone else
around white with shock or terror. His favourite joke was
directed at one person alone – his wife. It was simple but
effective. After she had been out in her car leaving him
alone in the house, he would wait until he heard the car
drawing up to the house, then her footsteps returning to
their front door. At once he would rush into the kitchen,
turn on all the gas taps on their stove, shove his head in the
oven and wait. It was such a laugh to see her shocked face
when he popped out alive and kicking. One day in 1956
Harry Winikus decided to play his favourite trick. His wife
took the car and went off to the shops. Half an hour later,
sure enough, he heard a car draw up, the door slam, and
footsteps on the path. He rushed to the kitchen and turned
on the gas. Into the oven went Harry's head, his body
slumped into a grotesque parody of a suicide. As the gas
poured into the kitchen and deep into Harry's lungs he
might have realised his fatal error. He didn't manage to do
anything about it. There had been a car, and there were
footsteps. The problem was that Harry's wife was still out.
The joke, as Mrs Winikus discovered when she came home
an hour later, was well and truly over.

Zeuxis *(laughed to death fifth century BC)*

It is said that Zeuxis, a Greek painter of the fifth century
BC, laughed so hard at a picture of an especially
unattractive old crone that he had just completed that he
was unable to control himself and the fit that followed
proved fatal.

The irony of it!

Abdullah Imam *(heart attack 1973)*

Abdullah, whose friend Murat Muletia, fifty-three, had recently died, had taken on the task of washing his friend's body prior to interment. As he poured a bucket of water over the corpse for the ritual cleansing, his supposedly deceased friend sat up. Utterly shocked, the mourners ran screaming from the house – except, that is, for Imam Abdullah, whose heart found the experience too much to take. A massive heart attack knocked him to the ground and left him dead. The next day Muletia, who had been assumed a corpse after nothing more fatal than an epileptic attack, helped bury his old friend Abdullah, using the very same coffin in which twenty-four hours before he had been laid out.

Allison Clay *(accidental death 1877)*

Allison was a Texan gunfighter who freelanced for the ranchers who fought each other to maintain their boundary rights. He was also an alcoholic. One day, on his way to kill one John McCullough, Allison toppled, blind drunk, under his horses' hooves. As the horses dragged the heavy wagon over him, it was probably of little consolation that he died with his boots on.

Anonymous Child *(drowned 1803)*

The following is reprinted in its entirety from the *Sydney Gazette* of 26 June 1803:

'A child, going to bathe in a deep pool, unfortunately went beyond its depth, and made much exertion to recover its feet, but in vain. A man, from a window, witnessed the accident, without emotion, or using any efforts to render the child assistance; but surely if he was not wholly destitute of every principle of humanity, he paid dearly for his coolness and unconcern, when he afterwards was informed that the infant was his own.'

Anonymous Diver *(drowned twentieth century)*

An expert diver and swimmer once volunteered to dive to the bottom of a canal from a bridge for a bet. Taking off his clothes, he executed a perfect swallow dive but failed to surface. When others dived in to search for him, his body was found perpendicular to the bed of the canal, with his head stuck firmly in the mud at its bottom.

Anonymous drug smuggler
(heroin overdose twentieth century)

A youth endeavoured to smuggle a large quantity of pure heroin from South America into the United States by sealing it in plastic bags and swallowing them before boarding his plane, with a view to evacuating the bags from his body after clearing US Customs. Unfortunately for him, several of the bags broke open in his stomach during the flight, and his bloodstream quickly absorbed enough pure heroin to kill several elephants.

Anonymous females *(choked twentieth century)*

A young girl asphyxiated herself by trying to swallow a whole rasher of bacon, rind and all. Picton records a case where an old lady who choked to death was found to have a complete rolled-up pancake standing on end in her windpipe.

Anonymous German glutton
(choked twentieth century)

An unemployed 37-year-old West German made a practice of eating in restaurants without paying. The police were still hunting him down when he lunched in a Marburg restaurant on an order of thick soup, herrings with onions and cream, shoulder of pork with cabbage and mashed potato, a large ice cream, three pieces of cream cake and seven beers. The food outlasted its eater: the ravenous glutton forked up a piece of crisp roast pork and choked to death where he sat.

Anonymous Glasgow woman *(shot 1908)*

In 1908 this Glasgow woman persuaded her reluctant husband to go downstairs in the middle of the night to investigate a noise. He took his revolver with him and, at his wife's suggestion, went barefooted to be as silent as possible. After he had gone downstairs, she anxiously followed him, carrying an unlit candle in her hand. Her husband heard the sound of her footsteps, suddenly caught a glimpse of her, mistook the candle for a revolver and her for the supposed burglar and shot her dead.

Anonymous London landlady *(burnt to death 1975)*

An enraged 71-year-old one-legged landlady tried for five minutes to run down her equally aged female lodger, in her petrol-powered invalid chair. The chair was not used to such excess and ran out of control, bursting into flames and killing the landlady.

Anonymous man

(choked on a mouse nineteenth century)

The *Illustrated Police News* records the case of a man who swallowed a mouse in a south London factory. The victim had just seized the mouse, which had frightened several girl workers, when it escaped from his grasp, ran up inside his sleeve, emerged from his shirt at the neck and jumped straight into his open mouth. He died very quickly in great distress. The *News* attributed his death to the mouse's gnawing his internal organs, but it seems more likely that the creature blocked his windpipe, causing death by asphyxiation.

Anonymous sword swallower *(stabbed in error)*

This performer made the mistake of bowing to his audience while the sword was still in his mouth. The act of bowing brought his upper incisors into contact with the blade, which broke off and slipped down into his stomach, perforating the lining and causing fatal peritonitis.

Anonymous woman
(killed in an embrace twentieth century)

Death can sometimes occur almost instantaneously when the throat is compressed, before the victim has time to be genuinely asphyxiated. This is apparently due to a reflex action of the carotid arteries that can stop the heart in its tracks. A case is on record where a woman suddenly dropped dead during a dance, in full view of numerous bystanders, when her dancing partner, a soldier, gave her neck an obviously affectionate and playful squeeze, lasting no more than a fraction of a second.

Baines Mrs *(shot)*

This lady of Chapel Street, Penzance, was shot dead one night by the watchman whom she herself employed to guard her orchard from fruit pilferers. She had made the mistake of sneaking into the orchard to see if she could catch him napping. She didn't.

Beenan D. H. *(hanged in error 1976)*

In 1976 Mr Beenan, one of New Zealand's most outspoken opponents of capital punishment, was demonstrating for an audience the terrible art of hanging. The onlookers, including his fiancée, Miss Bebe Trumper, watched spellbound as he slipped a noose round his neck and remarked, 'How horrible the whole thing is.' Mr Beenan then jumped from the chair and choked himself to death.

Bennett Arnold *(poisoned 1931)*

Bennett habitually pooh-poohed any xenophobic theories of Parisian water being anything but perfectly safe. To demonstrate this he downed a glass. He died shortly afterwards, poisoned by the typhoid bacillus that the water had contained.

Bernard Julia *(knifed in error c. 1890)*

A young singer and dancer on the vaudeville stage in late-nineteenth-century New York, one of Julia's roles was to be the target for a knife thrower. At her last performance, the latter successfully threw his first six knives, just missing her arms and head. The seventh was intended to strike the backboard just above her head, but the aim was low; the knife struck her forehead and penetrated her brain, killing her instantly.

Blanchard Madame *(killed in balloon crash 1819)*

Madame Blanchard was the widow of the pioneer balloonist François Blanchard, who had crossed the English Channel in 1785, and martyr to the twin arts of pyrotechnics and aeronautics. She was killed in 1819 when, during a balloon ascent over Paris, some fireworks that she had taken with her set fire to the balloon, causing it to fall from a great height.

Buckland Marjorie Gladys
(asphyxiated twentieth century)

Ms Buckland died of accidental asphyxiation when she was bound and gagged, with her active cooperation, by her husband during loveplay.

Busquetz Jose and Jaume Juan
(shot themselves twentieth century)

How the other half dies: Busquetz and Jaume were two wealthy playboys who obtained their *frissons* by playing Russian roulette in front of girls they had picked up in a Majorcan disco. One day the *frissons* proved fatal. First, Busquetz pulled out his .38 revolver, loaded a single bullet, spun the chamber, put the barrel to his head, pulled the trigger and shot himself dead. Jaume calmly picked up the revolver and, despite the agonised entreaties of the young ladies, repeated the procedure – with the same result.

Chipowe Lemmy *(killed self in error c. 1975)*

Chipowe, a Zambian magician, offered audiences a special trick. For one *kwacha*, he offered: 'Bury me alive. Wait two and a half hours. Then dig me up and I'll still be breathing.' It is not known how many performances were given of this act, but on the day in question Chipowe asked for and received his fee. He then lay in an open grave while members of the audience shovelled earth over him. Unfortunately, when they disinterred him at the appointed time, it was discovered that the magician had attempted his last trick.

Cockburn Alexander *(hanged seventeenth century)*

The hangman hanged. Cockburn was official hangman in Edinburgh in the reign of Charles II. He himself was hanged after being found guilty of murdering a beggar. In fact, being hanged seems to have been something of an occupational hazard for hangmen. Others who were themselves hanged were Edward Barlow, Ned Dennis, Pasha Rose and two men named Thurtell and Hamer who were hanged on gallows that they themselves had built. The wife of Roger Wilson, the hangman of Dumfries, hanged herself.

Curtis-Bennett Sir Henry Honywood, KC
(Heart attack 1936)

A distinguished English barrister, Curtis-Bennett was noted for his Falstaffian girth and his humorous after-dinner speeches. He dropped dead of a coronary thrombosis at the annual dinner of the National Greyhound Racing Society in 1936 while making a joke about his weight during an after-dinner speech. His father had died suddenly, twenty-three years earlier, soon after delivering a speech at the Mansion House.

Dodson Joseph *(poisoned 1938)*

Dodson and a friend, Cecil Hunt, were drinking together in a hotel room in Melbourne, Australia. After a few glasses they went to visit a woman friend. Hunt asked Dodson what they were drinking and was told 'poison'. He assumed this was a joke. Dodson tossed off another glass and challenged Hunt: 'You think you're so tough, have a drink yourself.' Hunt had a small glass and immediately felt ill. Dodson, undeterred, poured another glass but Hunt pulled it away. By now both men were in trouble. Dodson died on the way to the hospital. His cautious friend managed to recover.

Drexel Anthony J. III *(shot self 1893)*

Young Drexel, scion of a wealthy New York business family, was showing some guests the treasures of his gunroom. Picking up his latest acquisition, he remarked, 'Look, here's one you haven't seen before . . .' Drexel then waved the pistol at himself, pulled the trigger and shot himself dead.

Ellis Francis *(suffocated 1931)*

Ellis, a young Cambridge student, liked tying himself up, and developed considerable skill at this. One morning in 1931 he was found dead, bound and gagged in his room. His body was lying face down on some cushions. His wrists were tied behind his back and his legs and body tied tightly with all kinds of bindings, including handkerchiefs, cloths, flex straps, puttees and a webbing belt. He was gagged with a handkerchief wrapped around a sponge and his whole head was tied up in other handkerchiefs knotted over neckties, collars and a bath flannel. He died of suffocation, and it looked very much like murder or manslaughter. The forensic pathologist, Sir Bernard Spilsbury, however, was able to demonstrate that Ellis had in fact tied himself up in this incredible way while standing up, with the cushions placed on the floor in advance to break his fall and that, when he had finished tying himself up and had fallen on to the cushions, he had been stunned by the fall long enough to suffocate as he lay with his face in one of the cushions.

Falconer William *(drowned 1769)*

The eighteenth-century English poet made his reputation with a widely read and much reprinted long poem entitled *Shipwreck*. He died when the ship in which he was rounding the Cape of Good Hope was lost at sea with all hands.

Fierro Rodolfo *(asphyxiated in quicksand 1917)*

Fierro died in consequence of too great an attachment to his personal wealth. A general in the revolutionary army of Pancho Villa, Fierro took a short cut on horseback, straight into quicksand. He was so heavily weighed down with gold that he sank to his death.

Fiesco John-Louis *(drowned sixteenth century)*

This sixteenth-century Genoese count reaped the reward of his own murderous intentions when he set out by night to kill Andrea Dorio. Unfortunately for him, he lost his footing while walking over a plank between two boats moored at the docks and fell into the water, where the weight of his armour carried him at once to the bottom.

Foscue *(buried alive 1762)*

A farmer-general of Languedoc in eighteenth-century France died because of his miserliness. He kept his money, all of it extorted from the poor tenant farmers, in a secret vault to which he descended by means of a ladder. One day when he had climbed down to spend some time with his wealth, the trapdoor above him shut and he was unable to get out. The trapdoor was so well hidden that the searchers above went by without seeing it, and it was not until some time later that the new owner of the house, while having renovations made, discovered the secret vault. Foscue's body was found sitting amid his treasures. In his last hunger he had eaten his candle and some of the flesh from his own arms and shoulders before dying.

Hatal Michael *(shot 1899)*

A magician, whose stage name was Hungarian Hermann, died at an Oddfellows benefit show in New York in October 1899 when a bullet-catching trick literally misfired.

Hoffman Wolfgang *(killed by an arrow)*

Ten-year-old Wolfgang Hoffman was persuaded by his
father, a usually capable archer, to stand as a latterday
double for William Tell's famous son. Wolfgang perched
an apple on his head, and his father took careful aim, but
his skill failed to match up to that of the great Swiss hero.
His arrow went straight through the youngster's head,
killing him.

Houdini Harry *(punched to death 1926)*

The great escapologist died not during one of his
dangerous and death-defying stunts, but as the result of
the overzealous attentions of a fan. Houdini, who let it be
known that he could withstand any blow, however vicious,
to his belly, was unprepared one afternoon in 1926 when a
fan strode up and smashed a hook into his stomach.
Without the special tension that really did make his
stomach muscles well-nigh invulnerable, Houdini
collapsed in agony. Peritonitis set in, and Houdini was to
make no more escapes.

Ishmaelo Yousouf *(drowned 1898)*

This monstrous Turkish wrestler pursued a successful
trail across the USA in the 1890s, defeating such top-class
rivals as Ernest Roeber and Evan Lewis, both champions.
To ward off thieves and shysters, Ishmaelo would have all
his winnings converted into solid gold pieces which he
secured in a money belt that he never removed from his
waist. In 1898, as he set off home across the Atlantic on *Le
Bourgogne*, the ship collided with a British vessel off Nova
Scotia. As the captain ordered 'Abandon ship!' the
wrestler refused to be parted from his belt. Although he
was normally a good swimmer, the gold coins were simply
too heavy for buoyancy, He went down, still a rich man, to
a watery grave.

John XXI Pope *(crushed to death 1276)*

One of the most learned of the Popes, John XXI was already famous before his election, as a philosopher, theologian and physician named Peter of Spain. One of his first acts as Pope was to have a special apartment added to the papal palace so that he might have peace and quiet for his studies. Within eight months the new apartment collapsed on top of him, causing his death.

Kath Terry *(accidental death 1978)*

Kath was a member of the million-selling rock band Chicago. He died indulging his long-time passion for firearms. Brandishing a new revolver in front of the rest of the band, Kath started a jokey game of Russian roulette. When fellow musicians told him not to be stupid, he laughed at them: 'Don't worry, this thing's not loaded.' Then he raised the gun to his temple and pulled the trigger. It was loaded and a .45 shell shattered his brain. To add a tasteless irony to the whole sorry affair, Chicago's manager had only recently told pressmen who were following up rumours of Kath's possible departure from the group that 'The only way Terry leaves this band is in a pine box.'

Kirchman N. *(killed by lightning 1753)*

Kirchman was a professor of philsophy who died in dramatic circumstances in 1753 when one of his research projects proved all too successful. While endeavouring to attract 'electric fluid' from the clouds with a device he had developed for that purpose, a ball of fire from the heavens struck him on the head, killing him instantly.

Kotzwarra *(hanged in error 1790)*

As was his sexual preference, Kotzwarra, a London musician, visited prostitutes to gratify his particular predilections: bizarre and complex variations of bondage and masochism. On the fatal night, he first attempted to persuade a whore named Susanna Hill to 'split his genitals into two parts'. This she refused to do. She was prepared, however, to string him up in such a way that he was left completely helpless while she vanished in pursuit of more easily pleased clients. Unfortunately for the musician, Hill spent so busy a night, and had tied such ingenious knots, that by the time she returned he was dead of suffocation. Susanna Hill was tried for murder but, justifiably, the jury found her not guilty.

McClelland Elizabeth *(killed 1972)*

In 1970, 78-year-old Mrs McClelland left her native Belfast and emigrated to Christchurch, New Zealand. She told her neighbours: 'I want to avoid all this street violence.' Two years later, in February 1972, Mrs McClelland died in a Christchurch hospital from injuries sustained to her head. She had been hit heavily by a placard carried by a demonstration in favour of Irish civil rights.

McLaren Alan *(choked twentieth century)*

Engineer Alan McLaren, thirty-two, picked up a bar of chocolate and announced to fellow guests in an Australian hotel; 'See how long it takes me to eat this.' He popped the bar into his mouth and left the room. Later he was found dead of asphyxiation.

Oliver of Malmesbury *(failed to fly eleventh century)*

The English Icarus, Oliver was an eleventh-century Benedictine monk who was skilled in mechanical contrivance. He made a pair of wings, fastened them to his hands and feet and, leaping from a lofty tower, attempted to fly. He failed.

Overs John *(killed in error)*

Avaricious River Thames ferryman, Overs' single-minded greed and miserliness brought about his own death and, indirectly, that of an equally greedy young man. The latter was paying suit to Overs' daughter Mary for purely financial reasons, since Overs had accumulated quite a fortune, which the young man hoped to inherit through marriage. Overs devised a scheme to save a little more money: he would feign death for twenty-four hours, in the expectation that his servants would, as a gesture of mourning, fast until his funeral, thus saving the expense of a whole day's food. When, however, Overs was laid out on his bed and the news of his death conveyed by an accomplice to the servants, the latter were delighted and, instead of fasting, began to dance and feast upon the contents of Overs' larder. The bogus corpse was horrified at this unforeseen development and he sat upright to rebuke his servants. This so alarmed one of them that he struck out in wild terror at the supposed ghost with a bar of wood and shattered Overs' skull. As soon as Mary's suitor heard the news that his inheritance was so much closer, he set out post haste on horseback to join his young heiress; but in his haste rode carelessly and was thrown off, breaking his neck.

Robinson William Ellisworth *(shot in error 1918)*

Better known by his stage name of Chung Ling Soo, this famous magician of the early twentieth century was killed

on stage by one of his own tricks – catching a marked bullet
fired at him by a member of the audience. At his
performance on 23 March 1918 at the Empire Theatre,
Wood Green in London, a trickle of gunpowder worked its
way through a worn part of the trick mechanism within the
gun and ignited a charge that was never intended to
project a bullet – but in this case did.

Solomon Keith *(heart attack)*

Fifty-eight-year-old Solomon, of Ontario, Canada, died in
peculiarly frustrating circumstances. He had set out to
climb all forty-six mountains in the Adirondack range. He
successfully climbed forty-five of them and then died of a
heart attack when only 135 metres from the summit of
Saddleback Mountain, the forty-sixth and, in more ways
than one, the final challenge.

Stanton George *(crushed by an elephant)*

A boy was crushed to death by an elephant for feeding it
with a stone instead of bread. Stanton was one of several
children who were feeding the elephant at Bostock and
Wombwell's menagerie at Hanley. The others gave it nuts
and bread but Stanton teased it and tricked it into
accepting a stone. It picked him up with its trunk and
pushed him against a wall. He died of internal injuries
within twenty-four hours.

Stenbock Count Eric Magnus Andreas Harry *(killed self 1895)*

English nobleman and writer Stenbock killed himself in a
drunken rage when, attempting to beat a friend with a
poker, he slipped, fell into his own fireplace, and was burnt
to death.

Tchaikovsky Peter *(died of cholera 1893)*

The great Russian composer died of cholera, contracted after drinking a glass of unboiled water, to the horror of those present, during a cholera epidemic. As he drank it he said that he was less afraid of cholera than of other illnesses.

Telemachus *(stoned to death 404 AD)*

One of the nobler deaths recorded in these pages. Telemachus was a monk who, in 404 AD, leaped into the arena at the Colosseum and appealed to the spectators to stop the cruel sport of gladiatorial combat. (By this stage, most of the even crueller and more perverse spectacles of the Roman circuses had already disappeared.) He was rewarded for his temerity by being immediately stoned to death by the enraged mob. But he won his point; Emperor Honorius closed the arenas and they never reopened.

Valavoir Count *(shot seventeenth century)*

Victim of a fatal double meaning, a seventeenth-century French general serving under Turenne, Valavoir was challenged in camp one dark night by one of his own sentinels. The count answered by calling out his name, the literal meaning of which is 'go and see' (*va le voir*). The sentinel took offence at what he assumed was a piece of effrontery and, after repeating the challenge and receiving the same answer, he shot Valavoir dead on the spot.

Vincent Benny *(shot by a baby)*

Twenty-three-year-old Benny Vincent was showing his two-year-old son how to hold his .22 pistol. Then he showed him how to work the trigger. The boy responded eagerly, grasping the gun as his proud father urged him,

'Now son, pull!' At the inquest into her husband's death, Mrs Vincent described how she had heard the crack of the .22 and turned around to see her Benny on the floor, shot fatally through his head.

Webb Warder *(murdered 1888)*

At the execution of John Alfred Gell, in May 1888 at Strangeways Gaol, Manchester, the hangman James Berry was chatting with a warder, one Webb, when the latter, shaking his head sadly, said: 'A body never knows who will be next.' Shortly afterwards, Berry had to return to Strangeways to execute one John Jackson – for the murder of Warder Webb.

Wise Michael *(killed in a fight seventeenth century)*

A distinguished English musician in the seventeenth century, Wise was a composer as well as organist and master of the choristers at St Paul's Cathedral. One night at his home in Salisbury he lost an argument with his wife, rushed out in a passion and attacked the first person he came across. Unhappily for him, this turned out to be a nightwatchman armed with a billhook. With this he proceeded to defend himself, striking Wise in the process and killing him.

The higher they go

Adrian IV Pope *(choked by a fly 1159)*

Pope Adrian IV had just finished delivering a speech in which he attacked Emperor Frederick I and threatened the monarch with excommunication. Pausing to take a drink from an adjacent fountain, the pontiff sucked down a fly along with the refreshing water. The fly lodged in his throat, the Pope choked, and neither of God's creatures survived the meeting.

Agathocles *(poisoned 289 BC)*

A Sicilian made his way from rags to riches and became sovereign of Syracuse in 317 BC. He died at the ripe old age (for those days) of seventy-two, and is said to have been killed at the instigation of his own grandson. The story is that the latter arranged for a paralysing poison to be hidden in the quill with which Agathocles cleaned his teeth. The old man was then placed on his funeral bier and burned alive, being incapable of moving or speaking and thus unable to tell anyone until too far gone, that he was not dead.

Aeschylus *(killed by a falling tortoise 456 BC)*

The great ancient Greek tragedian was killed, according to Pliny, by the impact on his head of a tortoise that fell from the claws of an eagle flying above him. The eagle had presumably mistaken the dramatist's bald head for a rock upon which it could shatter the tortoise's carapace.

Agrippina *(murdered first century)*

Agrippina was the mother and victim of Emperor Nero. Nero took great pains to have her killed in a way that would appear accidental. His first plan had been to entice her into a night voyage on a ship that had been specially prepared to fall apart while at sea. The contrivance worked but Agrippina survived. Her escape was made easier by the fact that in the confusion one of her friends, panic-stricken to find the ship sinking beneath her feet, made the mistake of calling out that she was Agrippina – no doubt thinking that she would be given priority in any rescue attempt – and thereby attracted a deadly hail of blows from those on board the ship who were in on the conspiracy. Agrippina, more prudent, remained silent and swam to safety in the darkness. After this Nero gave up any thought of sophisticated methods and sent a band of men who cut her down in her bedroom. (Lest this story inspire sympathy for Agrippina, *see* Claudius, page 127). Agrippina had been told years earlier by astrologers that Nero would become emperor but would kill his mother. She had expressed willingness to accept the latter prospect in return for the former.

Alexander King of Greece *(blood poisoning 1920)*

This unfortunate monarch died at the age of twenty-seven from blood poisoning caused by the bite of his pet monkey.

Alexander VI Pope *(poisoned 1492)*

The Borgia Pope died in agony the day after he had accidentally consumed the poison that he and his son, Cesare Borgia, had prepared for a group of cardinals whom they had invited to a banquet.

Ananda King of Thailand *(shot 1946)*

The young king possessed a revolver with which he amused himself by shooting birds. When his body was found, it was announced that he had accidentally shot himself. Yet the bullet had entered his head high up over his eyes and had emerged from the back of his neck – a most unlikely path for a suicidal bullet fired by anyone other than a very determined contortionist.

Aquilius *(choked on gold 88 BC)*

Aquilius was a Roman consul defeated by Mithridates VI and ordered by him to be executed. He was killed by having molten gold poured down his throat.

Arach Colonel Meseura *(tortured twentieth century)*

Commander of the First Infantry Brigade in Uganda and one of the victims of General Amin's initial purge of top military officers, Colonel Arach was beaten to death after his penis had been cut off and forced into his mouth.

Aston Sir Arthur *(beaten to death seventeenth century)*

Aston was a Royalist commander during the English Civil War. When finally defeated by Cromwell's men, he had his brains beaten out with his wooden leg.

Atahualpa *(strangled and burnt 1530)*

This Inca chieftain was treacherously captured and murdered by the pernicious Spanish conqueror Pizarro. After the latter had extorted a huge ransom for the release of his prisoner, he condemned him to death by burning; but *as a reward for Atahualpa's becoming a Christian,* he allowed him to be strangled first.

Attila the Hun (*died on his wedding night 453*)

As King John died of a surfeit of lampreys, the mighty Attila – scourge of Europe and terror of the Roman Empire in the fifth century – died of a surfeit of women. In 453, Attila, as Gibbon delicately puts it, 'relieved his tender anxiety', by marrying yet another beautiful maiden to add to his collection of wives. The excitement of relieving his tender anxiety on the wedding night in this case brought on an aneurism, and the dreaded warrior-king suffocated in his own blood. His young bride was too terrified to call for help and his attendants too frightened to interrupt what they assumed to be unusually protracted, if strangely quiet, love-making, so the fact of Attila's death was not discovered until nearly twenty-four hours had elapsed.

Bacon Francis (*died of influenza 1626*)

Like Zwingli, Bacon was one of those few philosophers who died in the pursuance of their own principles. He was an empiricist and a pragmatist – at least to the extent that it was possible to be either of these during the reigns of Elizabeth I and James I. He died a martyr to the empirical method, having contracted influenza as a result of personally stuffing the body of a fowl with snow, in order to test the preservative properties of refrigeration.

Bajazet Emperor of Turkey (*1402*)

When Tamerlane the Great (1135–1405) captured his rival, Bajazet, Emperor of Turkey, he had him enclosed in an iron cage and put on permanent exhibition along with his wife Zabina, similarly imprisoned. Bajazet and his cage travelled wherever the Persian ruler went. After three years of this inhuman captivity, the Emperor and Empress killed themselves by smashing their heads with such ferocity against the metal bars that they died of the dreadful injuries this caused.

di Bandi Countess Cornelia
(spontaneous combustion eighteenth century)

The exact date of the 62-year-old countess's combustion is unknown, but when her maid went to wake her one morning, she was just a heap of ashes. Earlier, neighbours had noticed a yellowish, utterly loathsome half-liquid smoke pouring from the windows of her room. What the maid found was a pair of legs, in stockings, which were untouched, as were the cotton wicks of two tallow candles which had otherwise burnt up. Of the rest of the body nearly all had been reduced to ashes. The air of her room was dense with floating soot. Neither the furniture nor the floor was burned.

Baume Nicholas Augustus de la
(died of fright seventeenth century)

Despite the fact that he was proven in battle as a gallant and fearless warrior, this seventeenth-century French marshal was so superstitious that he died of terror when the contents of a salt cellar were accidentally thrown over him.

Bogolyubovo Prince Andrew
(strangled thirteenth century)

The fate of this capricious twelfth-century Russian ruler stand as a warning to all who think that personal safety resides in power. He was strangled by his own bodyguard.

Britannicus *(poisoned first century)*

Britannicus was a son of Emperor Claudius and thus a potential rival of Nero for the imperial throne. He was poisoned at Nero's command in 55 AD. As was the case when Nero's mother Agrippina had poisoned

Britannicus's father Claudius, the first dose of poison failed to work. A second dose was then mixed from a number of different poisons; judging by accounts of the victim's sudden convulsions and rapid death, the mixture probably included strychnine. A particularly cunning ruse was employed to ensure that Britannicus's personal food taster did not receive the poison. Britannicus was given a harmless drink which was served to him (after being sipped by his taster) while it was still too hot. Britannicus at once called for cold water to be added. The poison was in the cold water.

Bonaparte Jerome Napoleon *(died 1945)*

For the last of the American Bonapartes this was a sadly prosaic death. Bonaparte died of injuries sustained when he tripped over the lead of his wife's dog, which he was exercising in Central Park, New York City.

Buonaparte Napoleon *(?poisoned 1821)*

The great French general and emperor was thought to have died of stomach cancer. Nearly two centuries later, however, the technique of neutron activation analysis applied to some hairs found embedded in his death mask indicated the presence of traces of arsenic, thus lending some support to the theory, long entertained in France, that he might have been poisoned during his imprisonment on St Helena.

Castro S. Guitterez de *(stabbed by priests 1869)*

Castro, the governor of Burgos in Spain, was assassinated in 1869 in circumstances that were unusual to say the least: he was stabbed to death by a group of priests during Mass in the local cathedral.

Charles II King of Navarre *(burnt to death 1387)*

Known as Charles the Bad because of his murderous and treacherous deeds, this king's death was appropriately horrible. He contracted leprosy, and his doctors, attempting to alleviate the resulting skin condition, wrapped him in cloth that had been saturated in a mixture of brandy and sulphur. His page accidentally set fire to these wrappings, and Charles died aflame.

Charles VII of France *(starved 1461)*

The king starved himself to death slowly, in mental and physical torment, out of fear that he would be poisoned by his own son. It was widely thought that this was his punishment for having abandoned Joan of Arc.

Charles VIII of France *(fractured skull 1498)*

Courtesy, combined with an interest in recreation, led to the downfall of this monarch. While escorting his queen into a tennis court, he paid more attention to her than to where he was going, and consequently fractured his skull against a beam over a doorway.

Claudius *(poisoned/asphyxiated 54 AD)*

Given poison by his wife Agrippina, Emperor Claudius showed no sign of being affected by it. She became concerned that the poison may have been expelled from his system by one of the various bodily evacuations that accompanied his dining, and called in his doctor Xenophon. The latter guaranteed Claudius's death by inserting a feather down his throat, ostensibly to help him vomit. The feather may have been poisoned but is more likely to have caused death by obstructing the imperial windpipe. (One of the sons of Claudius suffocated years

before when his windpipe was blocked by a different
object – a small pear that he had thrown into the air to
catch in his mouth.)

Commodus *(strangled 192 AD)*

Roman Emperor from 180 to 192 AD, Commodus was
strangled in his bedroom by a young professional wrestler
named Narcissus, at the behest of Marcia, his favourite
concubine. Marcia had first plied him with poisoned wine,
to no avail. Her crime, if the killing of such a dreadful man
as Commodus can be so described, was prompted by
concern for her own safety at the hands of her vicious and
capricious master. One of Commodus's tricks had been to
display his archery in public by shooting cripples who
could not walk and whom he had dressed up like snakes,
with their lower bodies encased in giant snakes'-tail
costumes so that they could only wriggle across the
ground. Narcissus was subsequently thrown to the lions
during the reign of Severus.

Crassus Marcus Licinius *(choked by gold 53 BC)*

Like Aquilius, Crassus was executed by having molten
gold poured down his throat by Parthian soldiers. In this
case, the method of execution had a special point: Crassus
was an extortionate money-lender.

De Castro Ines *(beheaded fourteenth century)*

Ines de Castro was the mistress of Pedro the future King of
Castile when he was still an uncrowned prince. Pedro's
father, fearing the political complications that would arise
from what was apparently a mismatch, trumped up a
capital charge against the young girl and had her tried,
sentenced and beheaded. Pedro was broken-hearted but
waited until his father had died. Once he was king he

arrested the assassins and had their hearts torn out as they lived. He then had his beloved's corpse exhumed, dressed as a queen and placed beside him on a throne. Until he died in 1369, 'Queen' Ines sat on her throne and no one at court could avoid paying her due homage, kissing her hand, walking backwards from her presence and generally treating her as a living monarch.

Decres Admiral *(blown up 1799)*

The French naval commander who survived the blowing up of his ship at the Battle of Aboukir subsequently succumbed to being blown up on his mattress while he lay asleep in his own home. A trail of gunpowder had been laid under the mattress, possibly by one of his servants. The culprit was never identified.

Dolgoroucki Prince *(killed in cannonball duel)*

A Russian prince was killed in an extraordinary duel with an elderly general named Zass. The two men had agreed to fight a duel during a battle with the enemy, not by attacking each other in the usual way but by deliberately standing together exposed to the enemy's line of fire until one of them was struck. This they did, glaring angrily at each other, until a cannonball cut the prince in two.

Douglas William, Eighth Earl of
(stabbed fifteenth century)

This fifteenth-century Scottish nobleman achieved the distinction of being personally murdered by his king. His ambitious and autocratic behaviour led King James II to summon him to Stirling, where the king remonstrated with him over his conduct. When it became apparent to James that he was not making any impression, he drew a dagger and plunged it into the proud Douglas's heart.

Draco *(lynched seventh century BC)*

This exceedingly cruel legislator of ancient Greece enacted a penal code so harsh that, over two and a half thousand years later, his name still lives on in the word 'draconian'. He is said to have met his death when he was 'smothered by the populace' of Aegina, while attending a performance at the theatre there.

Duncan, Isadora *(strangled 1927)*

Unconventional in death as in life, the famous American dancer was strangled and her neck broken in 1927 when her long scarf became caught in the spokes of the rear wheel of a car in which she was travelling.

Edward II of England *(murdered 1327)*

Edward II was murdered by two ruffians who, to quote Hume:

threw him on a bed, held him down violently with a table, which they flung over him, thrust into his fundament a red-hot iron which they inserted through a horn, and though the outward marks of violence upon his person were prevented by this expedient, the horrid deed was discovered to all the guards and attendants by the screams with which the agonising king filled the castle while his bowels were consuming.

Edward V of England *(smothered 1483)*

The son of Edward IV, whom he succeeded at the age of twelve, died mysteriously in the Tower of London with his brother, the young Duke of York, when they were under the so-called guardianship of Richard, Duke of Gloucester in 1483. The general belief is that both youngsters were smothered in their beds by agents of the duke.

Elagabalus Emperor of Rome
(killed by his soldiers 222 AD)

Elagabalus was one Emperor who seems to have set out to give Edward Gibbon something to write about later in his classic *Decline and Fall of the Roman Empire*. He was a sybarite, who set himself up as a god and indulged his every whim to excess unsurpassed even by his predecessors as Emperor, and no perversion or pleasure was beyond his needs. As one commentator put it: 'Rome was at length humbled beneath the luxury of Oriental despotism.' In 222 Elagabalus met what some saw as a fitting end when he was murdered in a latrine where he had taken refuge from his rebellious troops. His corpse was then mutilated and dragged through the streets. Rather than a simple burial, the tattered remains were tossed wholesale into a convenient sewer.

Elizabeth I of England *(1601)*

The body of Good Queen Bess was, at her own request, not embalmed. It lay within its coffin in Whitehall for thirty-four days before being buried, and the gases created by bacterial activity built up to the point where, as the lady-in-waiting who was sitting by the coffin subsequently reported, the body 'burst with such a crack that it splitted the wood, lead and cere-cloth; whereupon the next day she was fain to be new trimmed up'.

Euripedes *(torn to pieces by dogs)*

The great tragic dramatist of ancient Greece, while taking an evening stroll at the age of seventy-five was attacked by a pack of hunting dogs belonging to King Archelaus and torn to pieces.

Fauré Felix *(1899)*

Fauré, the President of France, allegedly suffered a fatal coronary when attempting to enjoy the more interesting aspects of a specially designed 'sex chair'.

Ferrand *(beheaded 1795)*

Today's parliamentarians must be grateful that political controversy nowadays takes a less dramatic form than that which so adversely affected this member of the French National Convention in 1705. During a debate, one of Ferrand's political opponents forced his way into the Convention, beheaded Ferrand, stuck his head on the end of a pike and paraded around the chamber with it.

Galerius *(infested with lice 311)*

Galerius Maximinianus was Roman Emperor from 305 to 311 AD and a determined persecutor of the Christians. To quote Gibbon: 'His death was occasioned by a very painful and lingering disorder. His body swelled by an intemperate course of life to an unwieldy corpulence, was covered with ulcers and devoured by innumerable swarms of those insects who have given their name to a most loathsome disease.' The disease so coyly left unnamed by Gibbon was *morbus pediculosus*, literally 'louse disease'.

George II of England *(heart attack 1760)*

King George II died seated on the lavatory when a heart attack, brought on by chronic constipation, laid him low.

George Duke of Clarence *(drowned 1478)*

The Duke of Clarence was reputedly drowned on the orders of his brother Richard III in a butt of malmsey wine. Sceptics point out that a more likely death was the same drowning, but only in the less exciting waters of a bath.

Henry VIII of England *(multiple diseases 1547)*

The first Protestant monarch died as a result of the degeneration of his kidneys and, so it appeared afterwards, of the long-term effects of syphilis. All his children – Edward, who died young; Mary, whose bodily odours revolted her husband Philip of Spain; and Elizabeth I, who may have been barren – had disabilities, possibly the result of father's youthful excesses. But syphilis apart, Henry's health declined from 1526, when a jousting accident set off a crop of leg ulcers that would never leave him in peace. For the last eight days of his life he was unable to walk, so vile and painful were these ulcers, and he lay in his bed, drenched in the stink of suppurating sores as they burst and poured pus on to his bandages. He had, as the *British Medical Journal* put it in 1910, 'become a mass of loathsome infirmities. He was bloated in the face . . . his legs were swollen and covered with festering sores, causing an unbearable stench.' When Henry was dead, his coffin was transported to Windsor for regal interment. On the way, the coffin burst open and guards found dogs tearing at the remains. For those who enjoyed such things, this posthumous fate recalled a prophecy aimed at the king when hale and hearty: 'The dogs will lick his bones, as they did Ahab's.'

Herod Agrippa I *(eaten by worms first century)*

This grandson of a more infamous Herod seems to have reversed the order of the usual processes in the manner of his death, being eaten by worms before rather than after the fatal moment. See Acts 12, according to which he was smitten by the angel of the Lord because he failed to give God the credit for a successful speech that he had just finished making: 'And he was eaten of worms, and gave up the ghost.' Actually, this gruesome expression probably meant that, like Galerius, Herod had died of pediculosis, a disease in which the body is ulcerated and its tissues permeated with lice that come and go through openings in the flesh.

Irene *(killed 1415)*

Irene was a beautiful Greek girl who had enamoured the first Turkish Emperor, Mahomet I. So fascinated was he by this girl that he spent disproportionate amounts of time with her, letting more vital affairs of state go unattended. Gradually the Emperor realised that many of his counsellors resented this woman and her influence over his conduct. He had them all summoned, adorned Irene in her finest clothes and jewels and paraded her for their eyes. When all had accepted how delightful she was and were profuse in their apologies for criticising Mahomet's justifiable infatuation, the Emperor pulled his mistress towards him, held her hair in one hand, bent back her head and with one twisting blow of his sword scythed off her head.

Ivan the Terrible *(sudden collapse 1584)*

The murderous Tsar of Russia in the late sixteenth century died just in time to save the lives of sixty soothsayers who had predicted that he had twelve days to live. The enraged Tsar had threatened them with death if he survived the twelfth day, which he spent quietly indoors. Towards evening, without any warning, he suddenly gave a choked cry and fell dead. Some commentators have argued that he was suffering from the final stage of syphilis – which would help explain the sheer lunacy of his more ferocious exploits – and that this had affected the aortic valve of his heart, causing it to stop.

John King of England *(died of food poisoning 1216)*

King John is said to have died of 'a surfeit of lampreys', the latter being an eel-like fish with a sucker for a mouth. Presumably he succumbed to some form of dysentery, aggravated by over-eating.

John King of Sweden *(killed by a theatre audience 1513)*

King John of Sweden was watching a performance of *The Mystery Of The Passion*. Unfortunately for those concerned, the dramas contained in this life of Jesus Christ proved all too much for its participants. Firstly, the actor playing Longinus, a Roman soldier who plunges his spear into Christ's side, took his part too seriously and actually stuck a very real spear into 'Jesus', killing him on stage. As this stage Messiah fell from his cross, 'Longinus' smashed into the actress playing the Virgin Mary and floored her. He then lashed out at the thespian who portrayed St John, hurting him badly. So enraged was King John that he left his seat, rushed on stage himself and decapitated 'Longinus' with a stroke of his sword. The audience, who had been enthralled by the real-life dramas, duly left their seats, grabbed the spoilsport king and tore him to pieces.

Lawrence T. E. (Lawrence of Arabia)
(killed in a crash 1935)

T. E. Lawrence, soldier, adventurer, chronicler of the war in Arabia and mysterious hero in retirement, was killed in Dorsetshire in 1935 when he suddenly swerved and crashed his motorcycle when avoiding two boys on pushbikes. The motorcycle had been a gift from Mr and Mrs Bernard Shaw.

Lewis Frederick, Prince of Wales
(killed eighteenth century)

Lewis was killed when he was struck by a cricket ball.

Lon Nil *(killed and eaten 1970)*

Lon Nil was the brother of Cambodia's President Lon Nol. In 1970 Lon Nil was seized by peasants at the town of

Kampong Cham. They killed him, then tore his still warm liver from his stomach. Taking this organ to a nearby Chinese restaurant, they forced the owner to cook and slice it. Once prepared, the cooked human liver was cut into morsels and eaten ravenously by the murderous mob.

Luther Martin *(heart attack 1546)*

Luther, the pioneer of the Protestant Reformation, suffered from a mass of afflictions. High blood pressure, angina pectoris (sharp pains in the chest due to heart disease), bladder stones, chronic deafness for the last five years of his life (the result of Meniere's disease – attacking the inner ear) and continual and intense constipation all led to his death of a heart attack in 1546. It was apparently of great comfort to the reformer that he recognised every problem as part and parcel of Satan's struggle to stifle his efforts.

Marat Jean *(stabbed in bath)*

Jean Marat was stabbed in his bath by Charlotte Corday with a 15 centimetre kitchen knife. She had politely sought admission to see him on two previous occasions and had twice been turned away by his attendants. Her plea, 'I wish to put him in a position to render a great service to France', went unheeded. But on her third visit Marat heard her voice in the hall as he sat in his bath, and called for her to be brought in to see him because he was curious to see what she looked like. He was thus able to view her at very close quarters.

Medici Isabella de *(strangled sixteenth century)*

The sister of Francesco I and evidently a fast worker, Isabella was strangled in her bridal bed on her wedding night as punishment for betraying her husband. Oddly enough, another sibling in this unusual family, Piero, killed his wife Eleanora in exactly the same circumstances.

Murillo Bartolomeo Esteven
(fell to his death seventeenth century)

The great seventeenth-century Spanish painter, like his contemporary the composer Lully, encountered death while engaged in the practice of his art. He was killed in the church of the Capuchins at Cadiz when he fell from the high scaffold on which he was standing to paint his picture of St Catherine.

Octavia *(bled, suffocated and beheaded first century)*

Nero's wife Octavia was usurped in his affections by the pernicious Poppaea. The latter persuaded Nero to have Octavia falsely accused of adultery and subsequently executed. The manner of death was particularly cruel. She was tied up and all her major veins cut open. This, not surprisingly, put her into a state of shock, which in turn inhibited the flow of blood from her wounds; so, to hasten matters, she was suffocated in a scalding steam bath. Finally, her head was cut off and taken for Poppaea to see.

Orsini Cardinal Giambattista
(poisoned fifteenth century)

Orsini was murdered in typical fashion by Pope Alexander VI, father of Cesare Borgia. Alexander had Orsini imprisoned but told his mother that, if she paid enough for the privilege, he would allow her to provide food and drink for her son in prison, thereby protecting him from any risk of being poisoned. The mother paid up and took over the feeding of her son. Too late – Alexander had already poisoned him, before his offer had even been made, with the notorious *venenum attemperatum*, a slow-working poison which caused death long after it had been ingested. To show his innocence, Alexander called for doctors to examine the corpse, but before they saw the body he ordered them to record a verdict of death from natural causes.

Overbury, Sir Thomas *(poisoned)*

Secretly poisoned by the Countess of Somerset while a prisoner in the Tower of London, Overbury's death is noted for the diligence with which his murderess pursued it. First, she took out a contract on him by offering £1,000 to Sir John Wood to murder him in a duel. When this failed, she had him imprisoned and systematically poisoned. To make sure the poison achieved its end, she arranged for different poisons to be placed in all the different dishes that were served up to the hapless Overbury over a period of time. Arsenic was put in his salt, mercury in his pork, cantharides in his pepper and powdered diamonds, acid, spiders and various metallic poisons in other foods.

Paul Tsar of Russia *(Strangled 1801)*

Paul was strangled by three of his own ministers – Zouboff, Pahlen and Benningsen – in his own bedroom on 23 March 1801. They called on him as he was going to bed and gave him the option of abdicating. His refusal sealed his fate.

Pausanias *(immured fifth century BC)*

Pausanias was a successful Greek general in the fifth century BC who overreached himself by seeking to become King of Greece through plotting and treason. He was killed by being walled up alive in the temple in Athens, within which he had sought sanctuary. It is said that his own mother laid the first stone.

Pentheus *(torn to pieces by women)*

King of Thebes, Pentheus climbed a tree in order to watch in secret the revelry of a group of Bacchic women, but they found him and in their frenzy tore him limb from limb.

Perceval Spencer *(assassinated 1812)*

Chancellor of the Exchequer and First Lord of the Treasury, Perceval was shot dead in 1812 as he entered the lobby of the House of Commons. His assassin, one John Bullingham, then explained that he had intended to kill someone entirely different – Lord Leveson Gower, a former ambassador to Russia.

Philip II of Austria *(asphyxiated)*

This monarch was killed by too great an adherence to etiquette. During a meeting with his council of advisers, he began to suffocate because of the fumes emanating from a charcoal heater in the room. Although this was clear to those present, no one would undertake the task of removing the heater because the official who was responsible for it was not present and the others felt it would not be proper for any of them to do his job. The niceness of their sense of propriety cost Philip his life.

Poppaea *(murdered c. 60 AD)*

Nero's second wife, who was largely responsible for the death of his first wife Octavia, died during pregnancy when Nero kicked her in the stomach in the course of one of his tantrums.

Prim Marshal Juan *(assassinated 1870)*

Marshall Prim was a Spanish prime minister whose assassination in 1870 succeeded more through luck than skill. While riding down the Calle de Alcala, he was shot by a gunman whose marksmanship was less than perfect. The only wound received by Prim was in one finger, which had to be amputated. However, the finger stump became infected and the infection spread, causing his death within a matter of days.

Raphoe Bishop of *(shot c. 1850)*

Surely the only bishop ever to have been killed while practising highway robbery. An enthusiastic spare-time highwayman in the mid eighteenth century, the bishop was shot on Hounslow Heath by one of his intended victims. The story was covered up, save for a cryptic reference in the *Gentleman's Magazine*, which commented in ironic vein on the bishop's being mysteriously taken ill on Hounslow Heath and dying of an 'inflammation of the bowels'.

Rasputin Father Gregory Efimovich
(assassinated 1916)

On 19 December 1916 six men met in a private railway carriage in a siding near St Petersburg – two politicians: Purishkevich (head of the Russian parliament) and Basil Maklakov; two soldiers: Dr Stanislas Lazavert and Lieutenant Schottin; two aristocrats: Grand Duke Dmitri Pavlovich (cousin to the Tsar) and Prince Felix Yusupov, the Oxford-educated husband of the Tsar's neice, Grand Duchess Irina. The topic: the planned assassination of the Tsar's favourite, the dissolute peasant monk Rasputin (the nickname he picked up in his native village of Pokrovsky means 'the degenerate') started life as another drunken, lecherous illiterate who decided to join the clergy and milk the gullible. More successful than most, he had attracted the interest of the Russian court and apparently his healing powers had saved the life of the Tsar's haemophiliac son. His lifestyle had not changed in St Petersburg. A huge man with an overpowering personality, he changed only the quality of his wines and women. As favourite he soon gained many enemies. In 1914 a prostitute, Kionia Guseva, was hired to kill him. She stopped him in the street, asked for money and stabbed him as he reached to pay her. Rasputin survived, and Guseva ended her days in a mental asylum. Two years later, with Russia in chaos, pressured by revolutionaries from within and the German aggressor on the borders, Rasputin's power seemed more and more dangerous. The six plotters agreed: his death was a patriotic necessity. To save the state from any further scandals, it had also to be secret. On 29 December 1916, Yusupov persuaded the monk to come to his house. The grand duchess had migraines, he said, and asked that Rasputin's healing powers be used to help her. With Lazavert disguised as his chauffeur, Yusupov picked up Rasputin. For a while he was reluctant. 'You see,' he said, 'I have been warned that enemies are going to kill me.' But he came and was conducted to the cellar of Yusupov's mansion, where a table of wines and chocolate cake was laid out. Every item of food and drink was liberally dosed with lethal amounts of finely ground cyanide crystals. As the monk drank and ate heartily, the plotters waited for him to collapse. Instead he seemed to thrive on the poison. Yusupov despaired. He left the cellar and returned with a pistol. 'Get down on your knees Father Gregory,' he told Rasputin, 'God give me strength to end it now.' Then he shot Rasputin point blank and the monk collapsed. Yusupov ran upstairs to tell his friends of his success, and they drank toasts, congratulating one another before Yusupov returned to the cellar. There, to his horror, he found Rasputin very much alive. The monk staggered across the room, caught Yusupov by the throat and tried to throttle him. The prince tore himself away, losing an epaulette, and ran up the stairs shouting, 'Quick, quick! He's still alive!' Rasputin

ran into the courtyard, where Purishevich pursued him
and shot him four more times. Then all six fell on their
victim and clubbed him into the snow. Tied with stout
ropes and bundled into a sack, Rasputin's body was driven
to the Pterovski Bridge and dropped through the ice into
the River Neva. The commotion in the courtyard had not
gone unnoticed. The police were summoned by alarmed
neighbours. Yusupov and Dmitri were arrested and said
nothing. The police dragged the Neva and found
Rasputin's frozen corpse. To the amazement of the
conspirators, even ropes and the sack had not finished him
off. When the corpse was placed on the river bank it was
seen to have burst free of the bonds and raised its arms in
one final gesture of blessing.

Romano Alberico da *(tortured thirteenth century)*

This Italian nobleman suffered more for the sins of his
brother, the cruel tyrant Ezzelino, than for his own. After
the downfall of Ezzelino, who had sadistically maimed and
murdered thousands of his own people, Romano was
captured with his wife and children. He was gagged with a
piece of wood and thrown to the ground, where he was
ridden for a while as though he were a horse, by a spurred
knight. Pulled upright again, he was held fast and his eyes
were kept open by force so that he was compelled to watch
his young sons being cut to pieces in front of him. Their
remains were flung in his face, after which his wife and two
daughters were stripped naked, had their breasts and
noses cut off and were hurled alive into a roaring fire.
Romano himself was then tied to a horse's tail and dragged
around rocky pathways until he died. His remains were
fed to the dogs. His brother Ezzelino had got off lightly –
he had been able to commit suicide in captivity by pulling
the bandages off his battle wounds.

Scriabin Alexander *(blood poisoning 1915)*

The great Russian composer and pianist died in 1915 as a result of scratching a pimple on his lip, an act that led to the onset of blood poisoning.

Sirov General *(killed by snakes 1934)*

Chief of the Transcaucasian OGPU (the forerunner of the KGB), General Sirov was about to settle down to sleep in his bed at Helsingfors, Finland, when his feet hit something alien between the sheets. Before he could escape, the general was bitten by two poisonous snakes which had been slipped in to his bed by unknown enemies. He died at once. The snakes were returned to a local zoo from which they turned out to have been stolen.

Tiberius *(suffocated 37 AD)*

Emperor of Rome from 14 to 37 AD, Tiberius was suffocated under a pile of bed linen, hastily placed upon him when he showed signs of recovering from a collapse that his well-known successor Gaius Caligula had wrongly assumed to be fatal.

Verus Lucius *(poisoned 169 AD)*

Son-in-law of, and for a time co-Emperor with, Marcus Aurelius, Verus sprinkled gold dust on his blond hair so that it would appear even blonder. He died while accompanying his co-ruler on a journey to Rome by carriage. Some said Marcus Aurelius had served Verus with part of a sow's womb for dinner, having carved it with a knife smeared with poison on one side only, so that he could eat safely of one serving while Verius was poisoned by the other.

Webern Anton *(shot in error 1945)*

The famous modern composer was killed by an American sentry who mistook him for someone else. His tragic mistake haunted the sentry in question for the rest of his life: his health deteriorated and he ultimately died in a sanatorium.

William II (Rufus) King of England *(shot 1100)*

The second son of William the Conqueror met his death in a freak accident while hunting in the New Forest. An arrow shot by one of his companions, a Frenchman named Walter Tyrrell, hit a tree, from which it glanced off at an angle and pierced William's heart.

William III of England *(fell from horse 1702)*

Not the only member of a British royal family to have
fallen from a horse while performing an act of equitation
in public, but in this case the fall caused fatal injuries. The
horse is reputed to have stumbled over a mole-hill, hence
the Jacobite toast: 'To the little brown gentleman in the
velvet waistcoat.'

True but strange

Anonymous English criminal
(hanged eighteenth century)

In the eighteenth century the bodies of executed criminals were often left hanging in chains for the public to view. At Portsmouth one such body was left hanging from the gibbet for so long that it came to be used as a navigation aid by the Royal Navy.

Aberle Harvey *(shot 1977)*

Vietnam veteran Harvey Aberle threatened police with a
gun when they approached him as he walked around an
upstate New York golf course. Their response was to shoot
him dead. It was noted that at the time the former war
hero was dressed in a woman's wig, dress, brassiere,
petticoat and bikini panties.

Anonymous German carpenter
(impaled by ice 1951)

Working peacefully at his job, a German carpenter was
perched high on a roof when he was killed, impaled by a
freak six-foot-long ice-skewer that fell from the sky. No
proof was found, but such aerial icebergs can come from
the frozen wastes of airliner lavatories.

Anonymous German youth *(suicide 1978)*

This youth had been fired from a job of which he was
especially fond. Sickened by the whole affair, he decided
to make a personal, and final, protest. He went down to the
Berlin zoo, climbed unhindered into the lions' cage and as
the horrified spectators watched, unable to believe what
they were seeing, let himself be slowly eaten by the
appreciative beasts.

Anonymous honeymoon couple
(killed in an air crash 1966)

On 4 March 1966 a Canadian Pacific DC8 airliner crashed
at Tokyo Airport, killing sixty-four people. Among the
few and fortunate survivors was a honeymoon couple who
managed to continue their journey on board a new plane,
a BOAC Boeing 707. Only eighteen hours after their first
crash, and almost immediately after their second flight

had begun, this plane too plummeted from the sky,
possibly due to turbulence over Mount Fuji. This time the
hapless couple were not so lucky. They died along with 122
other passengers and the crew.

Anonymous Iranian bishop *(duelled to the death)*

Two Catholic priests in Tehran were desperate to gain
advancement to the vacant bishopric. When one of them
was elected by the church authorities the other challenged
him to a gunfight. The newly incumbent bishop was shot
dead.

Anonymous males of Al Massara
(victims of a vendetta 1972)

The *Sunday People* of 23 April 1972 reported that every
single male in the village of Al Massara, a small settlement
in the Nile Delta, had been killed, the end result of a deadly
vendetta that had begun in 1950. No one in the village had
the least idea of the basis of this decades-long feud, but
local custom meant that the women of the village took it
upon themselves to kill as many men – the sex who carried
out the vendetta – as possible, thus gradually cutting down
every male around. By 1972 the birthrate had been long
outstripped by the deaths, and the vendetta of Al Massara
collapsed through lack of human material.

Anonymous university sacristan *('executed' 1934)*

The sacristan of the University of Aberdeen was
unpopular with the medical students there. His faults are
unspecified, but a group of them decided one day to take
their revenge on this apparently unpleasant man. They
tricked him into joining them, dragged him into a room
where he underwent a mock trial, found him guilty and
sentenced him to death. He was taken into another room,

blindfolded and made to place his head on a 'block'.
'Execution' took place when his neck was flicked with a wet
towel. No one was more surprised than the assembled
students when, reduced to genuine terror by this
experience, the hapless sacristan promptly suffered a
massive heart attack and dropped dead before them.

Barnet John

Barnet had a horror of the anatomy student's knife and his
friends therefore arranged to dispose of his body in the
only way that would put it out of reach of the
bodysnatchers and anatomists – by burying it at sea. This
was done, but to no avail. The sea delivered the body into
the hands of the surgeons by washing it up at the mouth of
the River Don.

Bateman Mary *(hanged 1809)*

After the execution of this murderess in 1809, her body
was first exhibited for charity and then her skin was
stripped off and cut into pieces for sale as lucky charms. It
was never made clear why the skin of an executed and
flayed murderess should be regarded as bringing good
fortune.

Beswick Miss *(mummified eighteenth century)*

This eighteenth-century Manchester lady bequeathed a
large sum of money to Dr Charles White and his two
children on the proviso that her body should not be buried
and that Dr White should give it a daily medical check-up.
This was in order to ensure that she was in fact dead, not
merely comatose. After her death her body was left in the
attic of her house and Dr White and his family moved in.
Every morning until he himself died, the doctor paid a visit

to the dusty bedside of the gradually mummifying Miss Beswick, where he listened for the long-silent pulse and remarked on the weather to his unheeding patient.

Bierce Ambrose *(missing, presumed dead 1913)*

The acerbic writer of *The Devil's Dictionary* and of morbid and horrific stories disappeared in 1913 without a trace, as suggestively as one of the characters of his own writings. He was travelling in Mexico and on 26 December wrote to his secretary saying that he was about to proceed from Chihuahua to Ojinaga. From that point he stepped into the unknown.

Bogle Gilbert and **Chandler** Margaret
(unsolved murders 1960)

Bogle, one of Australia's top physicists, and Chandler were found dead of poisoning – both partially undressed, both covered with newspapers – on the banks of Lane Cove River, a well-known 'lovers' lane' in Sydney's northern suburbs, early in the morning of New Year's Day 1960. Their deaths remain one of the most puzzling of poison murders. No amount of police research, from local police to experts from Interpol and the FBI, could make any headway with the problem. Forensic laboratories failed to identify the poisons that killed them. The fact that both victims were associated with scientific and libertarian circles only served to intensify the intrigue that surrounded their deaths and encouraged speculation that the poison used was especially exotic. Some of the suggestions put forward included nerve gas, LSD, radioactivity, cone shell toxin, cyanide gas, blue-ringed octopus toxin and funnel web spider venom (this deadly black spider was found in the area where the bodies were discovered). Later, the presence of grotesque and

unaccountable wreaths on Bogle's grave added a flavour
of the occult to the mystery. The facts, to this day, have still
to be untangled.

Buckland Dr
(died after swallowing Louis XIV's heart 1905)

Like Napoleon's preserved penis, which appeared
sensationally in 1972, it was once possible to view the
preserved heart of Le Roi Soleil, Louis XIV. Donated to
the Harcourt family by a French cleric who wished to
thank them in this way for providing so much hospitality to
noble refugees of the Revolution, this heart, looking like a
piece of dried-up leather, was kept as a curious relic by
successive generations of Harcourts. One day at the turn
of the century, the Dean of Westminster, Dr Buckland,
was visiting the head of the Harcourts. The regal organ
was brought out to show the distinguished visitor. The
aged dean, moved no doubt by some scientific fascination,
wet his finger, rubbed it on the heart and then licked it
clean. Then, before anyone could stop him, he picked up
the heart and popped it whole into his mouth and
swallowed it down – it was never agreed whether by
accident or intent. It was assumed, however, when the
reverend dean died some very short time later, that his
bizarre snack bore not a little of the responsibility for his
demise.

Burton Robert *(died 1640)*

Burton, author of *The Anatomy Of Melancholy*, died quite
naturally in 1640 on the very day on which he had long
since predicted astrologically that his life would end.

Byrne James *(died 1783)*

James Byrne was a simple Irish peasant boy with one exceptional characteristic. Born in 1761, he measured some 2.2 metres (7ft 2½in) in height. As he grew older, Byrne became obsessed that his body should not fall into the eager hands of the surgeons of his time, all of whom needed human corpses on which to further their study of anatomy, and who vied for the opportunity of dissecting such a famous freak of nature. Foremost among such gentlemen was the eminent William Hunter, who staked his claim to the giant many months before his death by sending his number-one 'resurrection man' (in other words, a graverobber who 'raised the dead' for medical purposes) to sit, mute and staring, in the audience of each of the Irishman's shows. As a contemporary put it, Byrne was hounded by this death watch 'as Greenland harpooners would an enormous whale'. Consequently the giant arranged to be buried at sea in a heavy lead coffin. But his efforts were useless. When Byrne did succumb in 1783, Hunter bribed the men who were to convey him to sea. Only Byrne's clothes were buried in his watery grave. The monstrous corpse itself was soon in Hunter's hands and thence to a massive cauldron in which it was reduced forthwith to a massive skeleton. So speedy, in fact, was Hunter that he did not dare reveal his *coup* for two years, even to fellow surgeons. Then he placed the giant on show in a glass case at the Royal College of Surgeons, alongside his opposite – the Sicilian dwarf Caroline Crachami, who measured barely 50 cm (20 in). To complete his grim *memento mori*, Hunter also placed the cauldron in which he had boiled Byrne on gruesome display. Those who know Sir Joshua Reynolds's famous portrait of Hunter may have noticed a thighbone suspended on a background wall. It is the most enduring remnant of James Byrne, painted for posterity.

Chelini Mrs *(died twentieth century)*

When she died in the United States at the age of
ninety-nine-years and seven months, Mrs Chelini's son
August was anxious to give her the best possible funeral.
Mr Chelini's concern that his late mother's mortal remains
be preserved from the ravages of death led to a macabre
court case. Within a couple of years of her death, her body
was found to have decayed badly. Mr Chelini had been
visiting her crypt in Cypress Lawn Mausoleum as often as
five times a week, and had been worried by the increasing
population of ants and bugs around her coffin. Since he
had paid a lot of money to have his mother embalmed and
encased within a hermetically sealed bronze coffin, Mr
Chelini sued the undertaker for $50,000. He was awarded
damages of $10,000. A summary of this bizarre case is
given in Jessica Mitford's book, *The American Way Of Death*.

Curie Pierre *(knocked down by a cart nineteenth century)*

The co-progenitor of modern nuclear physics was run
over by a horse and cart; the last, desperate retaliation of
the old world against the new.

Desmond Countess of *(fell from a tree 1732)*

This energetic countess died at the age of 140 as a result of
falling from an apple tree she had climbed.

Federici Madame Othello
(stabbed twentieth century)

Madame Federici died when her husband, Othello, a
prosperous Parisian grocer, stabbed her to death with a
wedge of hard parmesan cheese.

Green Mary *(suicide)*

Mary Green achieved the remarkable feat of walking twenty-one metres and climbing over a gate more than a metre high after her jugular vein and both carotïd arteries had been completely severed.

Hamilton Alexander *(killed 1804)*

The celebrated American soldier and statesman was killed in a duel on exactly the same spot where his son had been killed in a duel not long before.

Helgesen Lief *(died twentieth century)*

A down-and-out from the Bowery district of New York, Helgesen made a final determined pilgrimage on the day of his death, apparently aware that his end was near. He had been a brilliant and successful engineer for many years until one day he disappeared from his home and workplace and moved to a Bowery flophouse. There he lived the life of a derelict for ten years. Then, at about ten o'clock one morning, in ragged and dirty clothes, he came up to the desk clerk in the flophouse and said goodbye, adding that he 'had to get uptown today'. He also said farewell to other long-term residents and set out for the city. During the day he slowly and painfully made his way through the streets, so dishevelled and wretched that a number of people stopped to ask if he needed help. To all of them he simply said; 'I've got to get uptown today.' By the afternoon, he had lost a shoe, his foot was bleeding, and it was taking him a quarter of an hour to walk a single block. Finally, at nine o'clock at night, he reached St Agnes Church, east of Grand Central Station. He sat down wearily on the steps and to someone who came over to help him he smiled and said: 'I've made it back uptown!' Then he died. Investigators found that fifty years earlier he had been christened in St Agnes Church.

Hirst James *(died mid nineteenth century)*

Hirst was a wealthy tanner of Rawcliffe, in nineteenth-century England. A well-known eccentric who preferred to shoot game while mounted on a bull, with a herd of pigs acting as setter dogs, he bought a large coffin when still hale and hearty, as a preparation for his eventual demise. This coffin was kept in his dining room and used as a sideboard, on and in which a large amount of alcoholic drinks were regularly to be found. When he finally died, aged ninety, his coffin was carried to the grave amidst a procession of sporting gentlemen, racing tipsters and a pipe and drum band. The coffin was carried by eight widows. Originally Hirst had offered a guinea a head for eight old maids to perform him this final service, but none were forthcoming despite all his blandishments. It was noted that the widows, less scrupulous, were deemed worthy of but 2/6d (12½p) for their efforts.

Holt Harold *(drowned 1967)*

In December 1967 the Prime Minister of Australia walked to a near-deserted ocean beach in Portsea, Victoria, and plunged into the surf, apparently to go skindiving, unaccompanied by friends or bodyguards. He was never seen again. The fact that Holt was an experienced and competent swimmer and skindiver, allied to the fact that his body was never found, has lent some credence to the varied and sometimes highly fanciful theories that have been advanced to explain his disappearance. The most likely explanation remains that the irresistible currents of an angry ocean had carried away yet another human being who had ventured too rashly to pit himself against them.

Howard Leslie *(died in air crash 1943)*

The British actor who featured in American films of the 1930s was killed in a plane crash during the war in the most unfortunate circumstances. The plane that was taking him on a secret mission was shot down by the Germans, who knew about his trip in advance. The tragedy of it was that the British knew the Germans knew, but were unable to give any warning because to do so would have alerted the Germans to the fact that their vital code had been broken.

Jacob John *(died 1790)*

A case of extreme longevity, leading to a pitiful death.
Jacob reached the age of 120, at which point he was sold by
his granddaughter to a travelling charlatan for 100
crowns. The charlatan took Jacob from town to town and
exhibited him in fairs and street shows, and the strain of
his way of life soon killed the old man.

Jippensha Ikku *(died 1831)*

The Japanese comic novelist and poet died in 1831. A
comedian in private life as well as in his writings, and a
great practical joker, he is said to have arranged in advance
to have fireworks concealed beneath his funeral shroud, so
that his cremation would go off with a bang.

Koch Mary Anne *(killed by roses 1979)*

When a florist delivered a bunch of eight red roses to Mary Anne Koch, she was overjoyed at her husband Michael's impromptu anniversary gift. But 28-year-old Mrs Koch had all too short a time to rejoice. She bent over the roses, inhaled their bouquet and then, as her stunned workmates looked on, collapsed and died. No adequate explanation has ever been offered.

Labelliere Major Peter *(died 1800)*

The major died on 6 June 1800 and was buried upon Box Hill. The manner of his burial reflected his disenchantment with current modes. He directed in his will that his body should be buried vertically, head downwards, so that 'as the world was turned topsy turvy, it was fit that he should be so buried that he might be right at last!'

Lake Mrs Stanley
(spontaneous combustion 1930)

Mrs Lake was mysteriously burned to death in New York in 1930 without the clothes she was wearing being so much as scorched.

Ledesma Catalina *and ten others (poisoned 1971)*

In 1971 Mrs Ledesma, a Peruvian peasant, fed some small cakes to her five children. Within an hour four of them were dead. Local authorities investigated and announced that a strong and deadly insecticide had apparently been mixed up with the sugar she used to make the cakes. The sugar stocks were duly destroyed. Five days later when relatives gathered to mourn her children, Mrs Ledesma served more cakes. An hour later seven more victims, including Catalina herself, were dead. Further analyses revealed that the initial theories were only partially accurate. A poisonous insecticide did exist, certainly, but the problem was that it had tainted the flour, not the sugar.

Murakami Shoichi *(killed and distributed in soup 1978)*

Gang leader Murakami ran the streets of Tokyo, until in the end the street, and those who lived on it, simply and literally swallowed him up. Victim of a long-running gang war that split the Tokyo underworld, Murakami met his fate when five assailants, each armed with a hatchet, surrounded and killed him. Then they put the knives to their original use when they methodically dismembered the former gang boss. The biggest bits were disposed of around the restaurant dustbins, but to make sure the police never identified Marakami's telltale fingerprints, his hands were cooked and served up, to the delight of more than fifty unsuspecting purchasers, as part of the savoury meat-and-noodle soups so popular in street-market food stalls in Japan.

Naysmith Robert *(swallowed metal 1906)*

Naysmith, otherwise known as 'the human ostrich', made a career out of swallowing the generally unswallowable – glass, nails, hatpins, stones and other such unpalatable objects. He died in an Islington workhouse, destitute and already ill. Born to a highly respectable Scottish family in Montrose, Naysmith somehow alienated himself from them and found a bizarre profession touring the country showing off his unlikely appetites. Inevitably such perilous consumption took its toll and in 1906, aged only thirty-four, he was forced to give it up. He eked out a precarious living selling bootlaces, but soon poverty and illness drove him into the workhouse. Unknown in his 'ostrich' guise to the doctors, he failed to convince them of the cause of his illness until an abscess formed on his body and on bursting revealed a brass-headed nail within. By now the unfortunate Naysmith was past recovery and he weakened and died in the summer of 1906. A post-mortem revealed an amazing catalogue of thirty odd nails and hatpins spread around his liver, kidneys and intestines. Medically, his death came through gastritis and peritonitis. The coroner's jury recorded a verdict of death by misadventure.

Nolan Captain Lewis *(killed in battle 1854)*

While leading his cavalry in the famous Charge of the
Light Brigade at Balaclava, Nolan was hit by a Russian
shell that tore open his chest wall, killing him instantly.
According to Ogston: 'The arm which he was waving in the
air at the moment remained high uplifted, and he retained
his seat on his horse, which wheeled around and returned;
the rider gave a death-shriek, and passed through the
ranks in the same position and attitude before dropping
from the saddle.'

Parker Richard *(killed and eaten 1884)*

On a visit to England, Mr J. H. Want of Sydney, Australia,
purchased the 31-ton yacht *Mignonette*. He hired four men
to crew the boat back to Australia: Thomas Dudley, 31, as
captain; Edmund Brooks, 39, and Edwin Stephens, 36, as
crew; Richard Parker, 17, as cabin boy. They left
Southampton on 19 May, crossing the line on 17 June.
Then violent storms began and the *Mignonette* was unable
to cope with the heavy seas. On 3 July they were forced to
abandon their waterlogged vessel, taking with them only
the barest of provisions: two cans of vegetables. These,
naturally, ran out all too soon. After several days at sea,
they managed to capture and kill a turtle, but the captain,
Thomas Dudley, failed to grasp their situation. Rather
than eke out the prize, they managed to devour it in eight
days and were left hungry again. On 23 July, Richard
Parker, mad with thirst, made the fatal mistake of drinking
sea water. Broiled under the sun, his mind started to
wander. The other crew members began a grim debate as
Parker sat oblivious. While Brooks, a single man with no
one to mourn him at home, disagreed, it was decided on a
majority vote to kill young Parker and eat his remains.
Dudley told Parker what he was about to do, then
dispatched him with a stab in the throat. The three men

started eating their erstwhile shipmate. On 28 July, twenty-five days after their ordeal had begun, the three remaining survivors of the *Mignonette* were saved by a German ship, *Montezuma*. On landing at Falmouth they admitted their lapse into cannibalism and were arrested. Brooks was exonerated, but Dudley and Stephens were charged and sentenced to death. The public outcry that greeted such sentences managed to influence the authorities. The sentences were reduced to six months' gaol with hard labour. It was the tale of Richard Parker that influenced W. S. Gilbert to write his ballad of nautical cannibalism, 'The Yarn Of The Nancy Bell'.

Parr Thomas *(killed by a change of air 1635)*

'Old Parr', as he was called, was born in 1483 and lived the life of a farm labourer in Shropshire until, at the age of 152, he was brought as a living curiosity to stay at the court of Charles I. There he soon died. His body was examined by the famous Dr Harvey, who could find no internal cause of death and attributed the old man's sudden decline to the change from country to city atmosphere.

Phillips Gwendoline *(suffocated twentieth century)*

This death is of interest because of the medical detective work of Sir Bernard Spilsbury, who was able to deduce from the victim's remains (found after eighteen months' exposure to the elements) that she had tripped and fallen face down in a patch of bog while running across a moor, and had suffocated before she could extricate herself.

Primarda Rolla *(killed by lightning 1949)*

Primarda was struck by lightning in 1949 while standing on the same spot upon which both his father (twenty years earlier) and his grandfather (50 years earlier) had been killed in identical fashion.

Reeser Mrs Mary *(burned to death 1951)*

Plump 67-year-old Mrs Reeser was found completely burnt to death in her home in St Petersburg, Florida, in July 1951. A highly localised fire, with no apparent source, had consumed her as she sat in her armchair. Investigating officer Warren Korgman said: 'Never have I seen a skull so shrunken, nor a body so completely consumed by heat.' He added gratuitously: 'This is contrary to normal experience.' What baffled all concerned was that the absolute reduction of Mrs Reese's body, by a 3000°F heat that exceeded that used in crematoria, had failed to make so much as a scorchmark on the room in which she was found. No reason for this apparent case of spontaneous human combustion was ever ascribed.

Renczi Vera *(the lovers of)*

The thirty-two gentlemen lovers of Vera Renczi, together with the Romanian murderess's two husbands and a son, were poisoned and kept in zinc coffins in her basement as keepsakes. She would sit among the coffins in her armchair after dinner each night.

Ryan Elizabeth *(died 1979)*

Elizabeth Ryan won nineteen Wimbledon tennis titles
between 1914 and 1934, a record that stood for forty-five
years. On 6 July 1979, Billie Jean King finally topped Ms
Ryan's record with her own twentieth Wimbledon
championship. That very day Ryan, aged eighty-seven,
became ill as she watched from the stands. She collapsed in
the clubhouse and died that night.

Sedov Leon *(probably poisoned twentieth century)*

The son of Trotsky died in hospital in highly mysterious
circumstances, at a time when he was hiding from the
Russian NKVD. He went into a hospital in Paris for an
appendectomy, and as a precaution used a false name.
The operation was a success. Then, for no apparent
reason, he was discovered wandering around the hospital
corridors, still in his pyjamas and quite delirious. He
lapsed into an unidentified fever from which he never
recovered.

Segall Ricardo *(died 1978)*

Venezuelan Segall was dancing in New York's 'New York
New York' disco. After twenty-five minutes of frenzied
gyrations he sat down, complaining to his partner that he
felt a little dizzy. He then collapsed and died.

Setty Stanley *(killed and mutilated)*

Dismembered by his murderer, Brian Donald Hume,
Setty was made up into three separate parcels – legs, body
and head – and dropped into the English Channel from a
light aircraft hired by Hume for the occasion.

Slatkin Mary *(infested with worms 1923)*

The pathetic case of this three-year-old girl, who died of worm infestation in Nettleton, an English village, at least served to bring to the attention of the public health authorities the first case ever recorded in England of chronic mass infestation of humans by the nematode worm. For several generations the local people had suffered from infestation by *Ascaris lumbricoides*, a helminthic parasite, but had accepted it as a minor inconvenience and never mentioned it to their local doctor, despite one or two deaths. Even when little Mary Slatkin died, it was a chance remark made as an afterthought that alerted the doctor to what was happening. Mary had been feverish, had vomited a good deal and had complained of stomach pains. The doctor had seen her, but when he returned three days later she was dead. He interrogated her mother quite intensively but it was only in a casual aside that Mrs Slatkin finally mentioned that Mary had vomited up worms. On being pressed about this she said the worms were like pale earthworms, about 20 to 25 centimetres long. When asked how many the little girl had vomited, Mrs Slatkin said: 'Oh, about sixty or seventy.'

Sterne Laurence *(died 1768)*

After his death, the famous author's body was stolen from Bayswater Road cemetery and sold to the Professor of Anatomy at Cambridge, for dissection at one of his classes.

Stuart Alonzo *(shot dead 1819)*

Stuart, a young lawyer of early nineteenth-century Illinois, mysteriously died in a supposedly phoney duel in 1819. His adversary, a farmer named Bennett, seems to have been quite innocent of any foul play, but two of Bennett's friends named Fike and Short may not have been so guiltless. The whole thing had been their idea. They had approached Stuart with a proposition that he should fight a duel with Bennett but that, unknown to Bennett alone, the guns would be loaded with blanks. Stuart agreed, and when the two duellists met for their encounter he was quite calm, while Bennett was pale and clearly in a state of trepidation. When the signal to fire was given, Bennett fired first and Stuart immediately fell dead with a bullet in his heart. In the ensuing confusion, either Short or Fike took Stuart's gun and fired it into the air; so it was impossible to know whether both guns, or only one, had been loaded with a real bullet. No one knew who had loaded the fatal bullet.

Summerford Major *(lightning victim 1932)*

Major Summerford was a continuous victim of lightning –
before, as a cause of and even after his death. Fighting for
the Canadian forces in Flanders in 1918, he was invalided
out of the army when lightning struck his horse and he was
thrown out of the saddle, sustaining serious injuries. Six
years later, fishing in his home town of Vancouver, he was
partially paralysed when lightning struck again. The
lightning hit him again six years later, and this time
paralysis was complete. His death, two years later in 1932,
was totally attributable to his earlier attacks. Finally, two
years after his death, lightning hit the Vancouver
graveyard where Major Summerford was buried and
shattered his tombstone.

Thibaud Jacques *et al. (killed in air crashes c.1950)*

By some quirk of fate, the late 1940s and early 1950s saw a
series of aeroplane crashes that tragically deprived the
world of music of several of its most gifted and best-loved
performers. Thibaud, the French violinist who formed
such a famous partnership with Casals and Cortot, was
killed in the French Alps while on his way to the Far East
for a concert tour in 1953. In the same year the brilliant
American pianist William Kapell was killed in another
plane crash. In 1949 the violinist Ginette Neveu and her
pianist brother Jean-Paul had been killed in a plane crash.
Indeed, the four years 1949 to 1953 were dark ones for the
world of music; also cut down in their prime in different
ways during this grim period were the pianists Dinu
Lipatti (33) and Noel Newton-Wood (31) and the great
British contralto Kathleen Ferrier (41).

Thicknesse Captain Philip *(died 1792)*

Captain Thicknesse, or, as he described himself on the title
page of his memoirs, 'Late Lieutenant-Governor of
Landuard Fort and unfortunately father to George
Touchet, Baron Audley', stood as one of the eighteenth
century's finest eccentrics. Among other things a one-time
'ornamental hermit', Thicknesse had pursued a long and
rambling career, mainly of a military bent, taking in
adventures in most of the known world and embroidering
it with long and absurd, but none the less bitter, feuds.
Accompanied by Jacko, his monkey, Thickness saw
neither rhyme nor reason as cause for moderation, and
few who encountered him came away unscathed. Of all
these, the man of whom he was 'unfortunately father', his
son George, was most loathed, although no specific reason
was offered. It was with this feud in mind that in his will,
read after his death in 1792, Thicknesse stated:

I leave my right hand, to be cut off after my death, to my son
Lord Audley; I desire that it may be sent to him, in hopes that
such a sight may remind him of his duty to God, after having so
long abandoned the duty he owed to a father who once so
affectionately loved him.

Thornton Charles *(heart attack 1916)*

Carter Charles Thornton was driving a vanload of timber
through the streets of London when he suffered a heart
attack and died. But by a grotesque chance, rather than
tumbling off his seat, Thornton was left where he was,
quite dead, still clutching the reins. His team,
unperturbed, continued to pull their load steadily along
streets from Blackfriars Wharf to Mile End, following
patiently behind another van driven by Thornton's friend
Richard Dean. It was only when they reached their
destination, a timber yard, that their driver was found
dead.

Townshend Colonel
(killed himself for science eighteenth century)

This early eighteenth-century gentleman claimed that he possessed the power of voluntarily suspending the action of his heart – in other words, of dying temporarily and then reviving. He submitted himself to an experimental display of this power before Dr Cheyne, Dr Baynard and Mr Skrine. Townshend went into a trance in which he showed no sign of breathing, heartbeat or pulse. A mirror held against his mouth and nose showed no trace of condensation. After this had lasted half an hour, the observers came to the conclusion that Townshend was in fact dead; but suddenly he moved slightly, his pulse resumed and he soon sat up and began speaking with them. Later that evening, however, he died permanently.

Turpin Dick *(hanged 1739)*

The famous highwayman, like many of his contemporaries, had a terror of his body falling into the hands of medical students after his death. He therefore went to considerable trouble to arrange for his friends to protect his corpse after his execution in April 1739 at York. This they did, and he was safely buried in the churchyard. Yet by three o'clock the next morning his grave had been dug out again and his body stolen by anatomy students. The townspeople quickly organised a search, and before long the body was located in a local surgeon's garden. It was carried on a stretcher through the streets, back to the churchyard, where its rescuers reburied it triumphantly, this time in quicklime.

Urquhart Sir Thomas *(died of laughter 1660)*

Sir Thomas Urquhart, or Urchard, was the first Englishman to attempt a translation of Rabelais. He also

specialised in mathematical treatises, such as the
Trissotetras and the *Logopandecteision*. A fervent supporter
of Charles II, he fled to France during the Protectorate. It
is alleged that so delighted was he at the news of the
Restoration of Charles II in 1660 that he laughed himself
to death.

Van Butchell Mrs
(the 'Preserved Lady' — died and embalmed 1775)

Mrs Van Butchell was the first wife of a quack doctor and
dentist, Martin Van Butchell, who was allowed by their
marriage settlement to have control of her fortune 'as long
as she remained above ground'. Accordingly, when the
lady died in 1775, Van Butchell, loath to lose his income,
had his wife embalmed by the same William Hunter who
would see off the giant Byrne (see page 153), dressed in
sumptuous clothing, placed in a glass-topped case and set
up in their once matrimonial sitting room. Here he
displayed her to visitors, always making sure to have them
greet 'my dear departed'. So popular was this exhibit that
Van Butchell, who usually advertised 'Real and Artificial
Teeth . . . from one to an entire set', was forced to place a
notice in the *St James Chronicle* on 31 October 1775,
reading as follows:

Van Butchell, not wishing to be unpleasantly circumstanced, and
in wishing to convince some good minds that they have been
misinformed, acquaints the Curious, no stranger can see his
embalmed wife unless (by a friend personally) introduced by
himself, any day between 9 and 1, Sundays excepted.

But for all the income involved, Mrs Van Butchell
vanished for good when her successor arrived. The second
Mrs Van Butchell had little time for so permanent a
reminder of her predecessor. The once famous lady was
tossed aside. It is not reported where.

Yeates Dr James *(unsolved murder 1960)*

A mysterious and unexplained death: Dr Yeates's body
was found in his Sydney garage early one morning in
September 1960. His skull was fractured, the injury
having been done to the top of his head. Near his body was
a pool of blood. The fragments of a smashed light bulb
were lying in the blood, and the socket overhead was
empty. He had a black eye. A small puncture wound was
found on his chest over the heart, and it seemed that he
had been injected with adrenalin. There were no holes in
his singlet or shirt, as there would had been had he been
given the injection through them. The forensic pathology
resources available locally were not able to determine the
cause of death and there the matter still rests. Death by
electrocution? By adrenalin injection? By a fall? A blow?
Murder? Accident? Suicide?

Zeno *(self-strangulation c. 290 BC)*

The ancient Greek philosopher who probed so acutely the
nature of time and motion is said to have committed
suicide by an extremely unlikely method – by strangling
himself.

All their own work

Anonymous *(suicide twentieth century)*

Pathologist Sir Francis Camps records a case of suicide by electrocution where the person concerned simply connected two rings, one on a finger of each hand, to the power supply and turned on the switch.

Anonymous American doctor
(suicide twentieth century)

A retired doctor in Oklahoma called a funeral home on the phone to report his own death immediately prior to killing himself first with a shot gun and then a noose.

Anonymous American male *(suicide 1973)*

One San Franciscan hippie found that his LSD trip, far from inducing peace and 'good vibrations', sent him into a hideous, berserk nightmare. Workmen stopped him leaping into their truck of wet cement, but nearby foundry workers were unable to grab him before he plunged screaming into a vat of molten metal.

Anonymous blacksmith *(suicide)*

A blacksmith wished to end his life. He charged an old gunbarrel with two bullets, put one end into the fire burning in his forge and then tied a string to his bellows. He placed the other end of the barrel in his mouth and, pulling the string blew up the fire. As the flames heated the gunbarrel the inevitable happened. The charges went off, and the bullets duly blew out his brains.

Anonymous Bristol solicitor *(suicide 1978)*

Many suicides from the West Country choose lofty Bristol Suspension Bridge as the scene of their final dive. However, the anonymous Bristol solicitor who plunged over the balustrade in 1978 managed a slight change in the usual tragedy. Rather than smash himself to pieces on the rocks below, a freak of wind, or merely the trajectory of his dive, took him down into the thick mud. Instead of breaking every bone in his body, he sank deep into the mud. When council workmen dug down far enough to recover the corpse, the cause of death was found to be asphyxiation.

Anonymous Englishman *(suicide eighteenth century)*

One English gentleman of the eighteenth century went so far as to advertise his imminent suicide. The event would take place in Covent Garden, tickets were available at encouraging prices, and all proceeds were to go to his wife and family.

Anonymous Englishman *(suicide nineteenth century)*

This gentleman, fallen on hard times, found himself bereft of his once indispensable servant. Faced with the concept of having to stoop so low as to dress himself in the mornings, he determined on self-destruction and, sure enough, hanged himself.

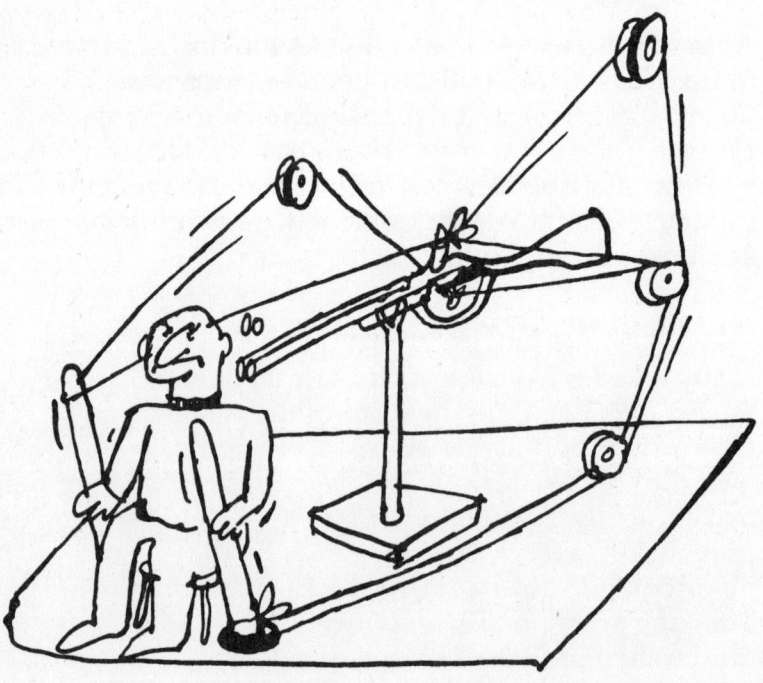

Anonymous Englishman *(suicide)*

Suicides almost never shoot themselves in the eye, the stomach or the back, but one enterprising individual in London built a complicated wooden framework with an arrangement of levers that he could operate in such a way as to shoot himself in the back of the neck. One wonders why.

Anonymous Frenchman *(suicide 1861)*

A convict at Brest died in 1861 from the effects of inserting a box of tools into his rectum. At the post-mortem it was found to be a conical box made of sheet iron, 15 cm long by 12 cm wide, weighing just over half a kilogram. It contained a 10 cm piece of gunbarrel, a threaded piece of steel, a screwdriver, a 10 cm steel saw, a hacksaw, a syringe, a file, five coins tied together with thread, a piece of thread and a piece of tallow. When inquiries were made it was found that similar conical boxes were in common use among the other convicts as hiding places for their possessions. The dead convict had made the mistake of pushing his box into place the wrong way round and had been unable to expel it.

Anonymous Frenchman *(suicide twentieth century)*

This Frenchman, having determined on a gaudy farewell, went to the Jardins des Rois zoo in Paris. Here he managed to scale the wall of the bear pit and jumped in among its denizens. Although keepers, alerted to the carnage within, managed to drag him out, the mauling he received from the bears proved just what he had desired. He died soon afterwards, apparently still exulting in his success.

Anonymous German *(suicide twentieth century)*

A Bavarian man was found dead on his lavatory seat, stark
naked, with a potato masher round his genital organs.
Apparently he had discovered that power from the mains,
applied through the potato masher, which he had shaped
to fit and wired to connect with the lamp socket, gave him a
special thrill. How he first discovered this is not recorded,
but he had developed the habit of regularly using the
masher in this way. All went well until the fatal day when,
having finished his recreation, he stood up before
disconnecting the masher, and in so doing took hold of the
lavatory chain with his hand. This proved a perfect earth
connection, and he was electrocuted.

Anonymous housemaid *(suicide nineteenth century)*

This unfortunate girl was accused of theft by her intemperate mistress. So hurt was she by what was an unfounded accusation that she rushed out to the wash house, immersed her head in a pail of water and held it under until she drowned.

Anonymous Italian *(suicide)*

Lost to misery, one Italian decided to end it all. His chosen method – setting himself on fire and burning to death. When, as the flames caught, he had second thoughts, he started frantically beating out the flames. So distracted was he by the pain and his efforts to counter it that he failed to stop himself plunging over a cliff and thus smashing himself to pieces hundreds of feet below.

Anonymous Japanese girl *(suicide 1976)*

Illustrator Edward Gorey told the story of a Japanese girl who married her American lover and went to live in his home country. Like many wives, she hoped to make her husband happy and, as an immigrant in a new land, was more than usually worried about getting things just right. Her collapse came at the kitchen stove. She had never even seen a rasher of bacon, but it proved to be her husband's favourite dish. Time and again she attempted to cook it, and equally often failed. In the end, distraught at her failure, the poor girl committed suicide.

Anonymous Japanese student *(suicide 1977)*

A fifteen-year-old Japanese student rang his mother and ended up in something even more deadly than the usual family row. Locked in argument over who should hang up the phone first, the young man committed suicide when he failed to convince his mother that it was those who received the calls, not those that made them, who should put down the receiver first.

Anonymous male *(suicide 1978)*

An anonymous man in Taree, New South Wales, intended to kill his dog. He took the dog down to the local rubbish dump, intending to do the job there. But when he came to it, the 55-year-old man couldn't face the task. Instead, he placed his gun in his own mouth and fired a .22 bullet into his brain.

Anonymous male *(suicide twentieth century)*

A man hanged himself from the roof of a tall building that happened to be right on the boundary between two different coroners' districts in London. The man used far too long a rope, with the result that the force of the drop tore his head off. The body fell into one coroner's district, the head into another. Considerable argument ensued as to which coroner should hold the inquest. The one with the body eventually took the responsibility, on the grounds that he possessed the greater part of the remains.

Anonymous male *(suicide twentieth century)*

A sexually disturbed young man electrocuted himself in the following fashion. He stripped naked, put on a pair of women's panties and a brassiere filled out with sponge rubber balls. Then he connected an extension cord to a power point, stripped the ends of the cord and fixed them to his nipples with sticking plaster. He connected a cord to the power switch so he could pull it on from a distance, and hung the end of his cord near a ceiling beam. Then he suspended himself by the wrists from the same beam with a cord noose, and while in this position pulled the first cord to turn on the power.

Anonymous Russian *(suicide nineteenth century)*

In the *Illustrated Police News* is an account of a remarkable late-nineteenth-century suicide from the St Petersburg *Zeitung*. The gentleman concerned booked into a St Petersburg hotel, where he locked himself in his room for the night. When the door was finally broken open next day, it was found that he had slowly roasted himself to death on his own bed. He had removed the mattress and laid on the iron frame, after lighting three large candles and fixing them in position underneath. His body showed little external evidence of burning, but his spine was found to be completely carbonised by the heat.

Anonymous woman *(suicide)*

This woman chose to kill herself by smashing a hole in the ice on a frozen pond. Then she pushed her head through the hole and held it beneath the frigid waters until she had drowned. Witnesses noted that no other part of her body was even damp, but lay clear on the dry ice.

Anonymous youths *(double suicide twentieth century)*

Two young men entered a restaurant and consumed a
magnificent meal. When the bill arrived they quite calmly
informed the proprietor that they had no intention or
means of paying. It had been a superb meal, exactly what
they had planned and one which their poverty would
never have allowed them to enjoy. In fact, so magnificent a
meal had it been that its only fitting finale could be death.
The *restaurateur* was suitably sceptical of such oratory and
let them go only after taking their names and addresses.
The next day, to check his suspicions, he went to see the
two men. As they had said, death would be the perfect
dessert. He found the two bodies lying, their hands
clasped, on a lodging house bed, hired apparently with
their last money prior to arriving at their last meal. The
corpses were already cold.

Bentron Frank *(suicide 1931)*

Guards on the Channel Islands boat-train uncovered a
bizarre mystery when they found a corpse and a suicide
note in one of the train's compartments. The last
paragraphs of a seven-page manuscript declared:

As before life, so after life, a return to the negative. The
conditions of pre-life have become desirable. Therefore I will
commit suicide. I am an atheist. Therefore I desire no service.
My body is fundamentally a mass of cells; because it is so, respect
towards it is unplaced. I desire that my remains shall be cremated
and the ashes mixed with those of the furnace. In other words, I
do not wish to be disposed of in any manner which indicates that
universal folly, 'corpse worship'. Yours sincerely, F. W. Bentron
– no fixed address. PS: You will find sufficient money in my
possession to make payment of five guineas to the Cremation
Society and this sum will ensure cremation.

Next to the corpse was an electric pistol, firing a steel
bullet. Experts decided that the projectile, about the size
and shape of a lead pencil, had been fired directly down

through the top of the head. The coroner refused to honour Bentron's last request, since no identification of the suicide had been made, and remarked on his surprise that a man so devoid of interest in an afterlife still worried as to the disposal of his remains.

Blaj Imra and **Stachitch** Mizzi *(suicide pact 1906)*

To quote verbatim from the *Daily News* of 26 June 1906:

A tale of horror which might figure in the repertoire of Grand Guignol is reported here from Belgrade. Two young people, aged 18, Imra Blaj, son of a wealthy tradesman, and Mizzi Stachitch, a butcher's daughter, whose union was opposed by their parents, decided to commit suicide . . . they went together into the country, descended a railway embankment, and threw themselves before an engine. The young man was dragged several yards by the cowcatcher of the engine and torn to pieces. His sweetheart was decapitated and her head thrown through the window of a cabin in which the wife of the keeper of the level crossing was playing with her children. The woman, seized with horror, snatched her two infants to her bosom and fell dead of shock.

Bruck Prof. Leo *(suicide 1928)*

Professor Bruck was lecturing as usual to his classics class at a Budapest grammar school. Telling with much enthusiasm and approval of the equanimity with which the philosopher Socrates had downed his obligatory glass of poisonous hemlock, Professor Bruck lifted a glass of what was supposedly water and drank it. He continued to speak for a few more minutes, then collapsed unconscious to the floor. His pupils raised the alarm but medical help came too late. Laboratory analysis of the professor's glass of 'water' proved it to be a most efficacious poison.

Buckley John G. 'Buck' *(suicide 1977)*

John Buckley, of Brisbane, Australia, 'Buck' to his friends, worried incessantly that the police were after him. In 1974 he had been sentenced to two months' gaol, fined $250 and disqualified from driving for two years, after pleading guilty to a drunk-driving charge. Due to an anomaly in the courts, no warrant was ever issued for his arrest, despite the sentence. For three years Buckley kept a bag packed with toothbrush and similar necessities for his time in gaol, but the police never arrived. Then in February 1977, 47-year-old Buckley cracked: he shot himself dead rather than suffer the strain of waiting one day longer.

Campbell John *(suicide eighteenth century)*

Campbell, a retired sailor, had settled on the Isle of Skye amongst his family. After some few months ashore, he was accused by a local woman of being the father of her unborn child. Campbell refused, whether justifiably or not, to admit this charge, and so incensed was he that he killed the woman to stop her accusations. Despite a hue and cry, Campbell was able to escape detection and capture. He fled Skye to Dumfries, where for a number of years he worked in farming, and began to believe that he would never need to atone for his crime. But his peace of mind was not to last. One day Campbell saw two old friends from Skye. Whether correctly or not, he was convinced that they were bound to report his presence and his crime to the authorities. To avoid the misery of trial and doubtless execution, he decided on suicide. First he took a gardener's knife and cut his throat. When this proved too shallow a cut to finish his life, he bound up his left arm very tight and cut it almost right through to the elbow. This failed as well. He then slashed at his upper arm as deeply as he could and thrust the knife into his side. The accumulated blows finally killed him and he confessed everything to a fellow Highlander who tended him on his deathbed.

Castlereagh Robert Stewart, Viscount *(suicide 1822)*

This famous British Foreign Secretary killed himself in 1822 by cutting his throat with a penknife in the dressing-room of his home after a mental breakdown caused by overwork.

Charondas *(suicide c. 500 BC)*

A lawgiver in southern Italy about 500 BC committed suicide on a point of principle. One of his own laws forbade the wearing of weapons in the public assembly, but one day he absentmindedly entered the assembly wearing his sword. When a citizen drew his attention to the fact that he had broken his own law, he immediately swore in the name of Zeus that he would re-establish the law – which he did on the spot by fatally stabbing himself with the offending weapon.

Christian Dennis *(suicide 1975)*

Dennis Christian was a devout believer in God. In order to prove that God would save him in respect for his great faith, he stepped blithely from the balcony of his thirteenth-floor London flat. A coroner's inquest was informed that the aptly named Christian's faith had not, in this world at least, proved particularly efficacious.

Chubbuck Christine *(suicide on television 1974)*

Twenty-nine-year-old Christine Chubbuck was a regular newsreader and the host of Miami WXLT-TV's *Sun Coast Digest* show. For more than twelve months her news-digest show had gone out, relatively uneventfully. One night in July 1974, as her next guest, a meteorologist, waited to regale the viewers with facts on weather forecasting equipment, Ms Chubbuck faced the camera and calmly stated: 'In keeping with Channel 40's policy of bringing you the latest in blood and guts, you're going to see another first, an attempted suicide.' She then produced a .38 revolver, raised it to her right temple and, before cameramen or her guest could stop her, pulled the trigger. Viewers saw her slump across the desk before the screen went blank. She died fourteen hours later without regaining consciousness. A *Sun Coast Digest* executive who checked her script found the suicide neatly included in her night's schedule. The shooting scenario was written in the third person and her condition after the shooting was promised to be 'critical'.

Cooper Herbert *(suicide 1911)*

Cooper lay down on the Great Northern railway line between Crouch End and Highgate in London in 1911, placed his neck on the rail and simply waited. He had previously murdered George Sanger, a famous circus showman known as Lord George.

Corbett-Smith Major Arthur *(suicide 1945)*

A former BBC official and author, 65-year-old Corbett-Smith was well known for his advocacy of the theory that all those of sixty and over 'whose continued existence does not in some measure benefit the community' should be dispatched at once in 'the lethal chamber'. He matched words with action one afternoon in 1945 when he walked on to Margate Promenade, lay down and placed a Union Jack on his head before shooting himself dead. Prior to his suicide he had posted a letter to the local chief of police. Headed 'Corbett-Smith on his self-dispatch'; it was duly read into the records at the coroner's inquest.

Crane Hart *(suicide 1932)*

This American poet killed himself in 1932 at the age of
thirty-three by jumping into the Caribbean from the stern
of the SS *Orizaba* while *en route* from Vera Cruz to New
York.

Dekker Albert *(suicide 1968)*

Albert Dekker, one-time Hollywood star, was sixty-two
when he decided to end it all. His career had been
successful enough. He had starred as 'Dr Cyclops' and in
top movies like *East of Eden, Suddenly Last Summer, The Wild
Bunch* and many others. But now he had little work, what
there was brought him poor notices, and his taste for life
had gone for good. Eight years earlier he had already been
bemoaning his fate. 'The theatre is a horrible place to earn
a living,' he announced. 'They sit you on a shelf for years
and then they take you and brush you off and later you
have to find your way back to that shelf.' Now he decided to
plunge from the shelf for ever. Dressed in his favourite
costume, women's lingerie, made of luxurious silk, Dekker
managed to tie himself up, arrange a noose round his
neck, snap his wrists into a pair of handcuffs, then hang
himself. As a last, despairing gesture, he had printed his
final, depressing notices on his body in a lurid pink lipstick.

De Nerval Gerard *(suicide 1855)*

De Nerval, a French Romantic writer, killed himself by
hanging from a lamp-post by an apron string.

Dessler Mollie *(suicide 1908)*

Mollie Dessler of New York was deserted by her husband
in 1906. In her misery she tried to commit suicide by
swallowing needles. Over a short period she downed 154

and was admitted to hospital in agony. It took twenty-six operations, many using strong magnets, to extract all but twenty of the needles from her abdomen, back, hands and nose. Those that remained defeated the surgeons, but she seemed out of pain and quite able to continue her life. But thirteen months later, in January 1908, one of those needles made its way towards her heart. When it reached journey's end it penetrated the heart, and she was dead.

Dodge Leonard *(suicide 1976)*

Dodge, a British Rail ganger, hanged himself because, it was alleged at the inquest, he was worried about metrication.

Duck Stephen *(suicide eighteenth century)*

This somewhat inappropriately named eighteenth-century English poet committed suicide by drowning himself.

Dugan *(suicide 1938)*

Dugan was a millionaire of apparently the most luridly melodramatic villainy. His business methods were only marginally honest, his general appetites so gross as to be, in a word, porcine. He over-reached himself when, seeking to force his attentions on one young woman, he found himself refused and chose to attack those around her. He deliberately destroyed her father's business. Next he turned to her boyfriend, ruining him and driving his father to suicide. Throughout this ruthless campaign, he continued to press his attentions on the girl, who resolutely refused his every advance. Then she and her boyfriend moved on to the offensive. Gathering together everyone whom they knew had suffered at the millionaire's whim, the couple arranged to have him sent literally hundreds of pictures of pigs. They arrived daily, by post, in parcels, by hand. There was even a large oil painting, in which a pig's leering head had been substituted by a human one, obviously that of Mr Dugan. Finally Dugan cracked. In an office surrounded by pig pictures, he shot himself.

Entwhistle Peg *(attempted suicide 1935)*

One of the thousands of pretty hopefuls who flocked to Hollywood in the 1930s, starlet Peg Entwhistle never made it. Her one role, in *Thirteen Women*, was insignificant and led her nowhere. Rather than accepting life among the losers, she chose to end it all. Her farewell lacked nothing of symbolism. She climbed Mount Lee to the giant sign that spelt out Hollywoodland, the sole reminder of Mack Sennett's ill-starred real-estate venture of the same name. She scaled the thirteenth letter, a memorial perhaps to her fragmentary film career. She stripped off her clothes, stood naked for an instant, then plunged into oblivion. Alas, even in suicide Peg Entwhistle proved a failure. Her leap for death ended in a clump of spincy cacti. It took her three days of agony in a hospital bed before she was finally granted release.

Falck Paul *(suicide 1930)*

The ultimate in Prussian drill and discipline was known as *Kadavergehorsam* – the absolute obedience and physical rigidity of a corpse. It was doubtless in this tradition that Sergeant Paul Falck, twenty-seven, of the Reichswehr, made this entry in the company record book: 'At ten minutes after midnight Sergeant Falck committed suicide by shooting himself. Corporal Junker has been instructed to take over the reveille.'

Forman Colin *(suicide 1977)*

Forman was a light aircraft pilot who had been eased out of his position with the Australian firm Connair in early 1976 and who had difficulty finding other work throughout the ensuing year. In January 1977 he smashed all his furniture and other possessions, wrote a letter to the Department of Transport saying what he was going to do, and flew from Mount Isa to Alice Springs. On arrival at Alice Springs Airport, he deliberately flew his plane into the Connair office building, killing himself and three office workers. He had sent the Connair staff a greeting card on which he had written: 'The end shall come a year after the beginning – beware the shadow in the sky.'

Fuentes Don Pedro Henriquez d'Azevedo, Count *(suicide 1643)*

Count Don Pedro was a Spanish general and statesman who died in battle in 1643 at the age of eighty-two. Too old and gout-ridden to make his own way into battle, he insisted on being carried in a chair into the midst of the fighting, where he was cut down.

Furnace Samuel J. *(suicide)*

Furnace is unique in the annals of suicide in that he succeeded in killing himself while under arrest in a police cell (for the murder of one Walter Spatchett) by drinking the contents of a bottle of hydrochloric acid that he had taken with him into custody, sewn into the lining of his overcoat.

Goering Hermann *(suicide 1946)*

The poison with which Goering committed suicide on 16 October 1946, just before he was due to be executed by hanging, had been concealed under a false navel.

Grenoble Bishop of *(suicide)*

A Bishop of Grenoble, having determined on suicide, chose an ingenious method. He took down from his four-poster bed the rod on which the curtains were hanging. He then suspended this rod across a stick which was linked to the trigger of his fowling gun. He sat down, put his legs either side of the rod and placed the gun's barrel in his mouth. When he dropped a leg on the rod, the pressure hit the stick which in turn activated the trigger and the gun went off, putting three bullets into his brain.

Grynes Henry *(suicide twentieth century)*

Hard though it may seem, American Mr Grynes managed to kill himself by smashing his own skull. Grynes was delirious and desperate to restore his right senses. To do this he decided to perform instant brain surgery. He smashed his skull with a stone, pulled aside a portion of bone two inches long by three broad and then stuck his fingers inside the cavity to tear away a large proportion of his brain. To his dubious credit, this 'operation' actually stopped the delirium and Mr Grynes returned home. He explained, most apologetically, just what he had done, and spent the next forty-eight hours peacefully and rationally with his wife and children. Not so surprisingly, those hours were the limit of his survival and he died on the second night.

Gunn Stephen *(suicide 1976)*

Stephen Gunn, twenty-three, a motor mechanic in Sussex, began to doubt his skill at his job. When in 1976 the same car kept coming back to his garage for more and more repairs he became convinced of his inadequacy. He threw himself to death from the ninth storey of a local building.

Hai Lin General *(suicide 1842)*

Tartar general Hai Lin found himself defeated in the
Opium Wars by British general Sir Henry Pottinger.
Faced with the shame of this disaster. Hai Lin built a huge
pile of his official papers, seated himself at the summit and
set fire to the paper mountain. He burnt to death,
although his conqueror, on hearing the news, said that Hai
Lin was 'worthy of a nobler and a better fate'.

Hall William G. *(suicide twentieth century)*

Hall killed himself by driving an electric power-drill no less
than eight times through his skull into his brain. Whether
this was straightforward suicide or a misguided attempt to
ease the pressures within his skull is unknown.

Harald S. *(suicide twentieth century)*

Harald was drinking brandy and soda with a couple of
friends in a bar in Nachtigall Square, Wedding, Berlin.
Although his friends grew increasingly cheery, Harold
stayed morose and silent. Finally, he turned to one of his.
friends and told him: 'Now I'm going to kill myself.' Drunk
as they were, neither companion believed him, and when
Harald stood up and left the bar, they made no attempt to
stop him. He went out, walked along to his own house,
lifted up a manhole cover and plunged in head-first. By
the time the fire brigade were alerted and dragged him out
by the legs, Harald was dead – drowned in the rushing
sewer.

Harden-Hickey James A. *(suicide 1898)*

Harden-Hickey was the self-proclaimed king of the island
of Trinidad. Of mixed Irish and French blood, fascinated
as a child by the glamour of the French court and married

to a Standard Oil heiress, Harden-Hickey announced to
the world in 1893 his decision to 'found a nation' on
Trinidad, which he insisted was an 'independent state'. So
besotted was he with his idea that he had stamps printed
and regularly paraded in a home-made crown. This
Trinidad, it should be noted, was not the larger West
Indian island, but a tiny (60 sq mile) islet off the Brazilian
coast. Not surprisingly neither the British, who seized
Trinidad in 1895, nor the Brazilians, to whom they ceded
it a year later, had any time for his fantasies. Among his
other pursuits was a belief in euthanasia, and he developed
the theory that suicide was a 'privilege', developing his
ideas in his book *Euthanasia: The Aesthetics Of Suicide*.
Among other suggestions, he named 88 fatal poisons and
51 instruments with which to end one's life. Depressed
after his failure to lord it in Trinidad, he asked his rich
father-in-law for funds to mount an expedition against
Britain. These were refused. He tried to sell his ranch in
Mexico, but found no takers. Finally, true to his theory, he
embraced the one privilege to which anyone, fake prince
or real pauper, could claim a right: suicide. For all his
multiple methods, he chose a very simple and painless one
– a massive overdose of morphine.

Herko Freddy *(suicide c.1970)*

A member of the Andy Warhol entourage, Herko was a
dancer and a heavy amphetamine user. One day he went
to a friend's fifth-floor apartment in Greenwich Village,
made everyone leave the room, put a record of Mozart's
Coronation Mass on the hi-fi and, at the Sanctus, danced
straight out of the window 'with a leap so huge he was
carried halfway down the block on to Cornelia Street five
storeys below'.

Holt Herman *(suicide 1978)*

Holt, a 55-year-old chip-shop owner of Halifax, Australia, worried obsessively about his income tax. When he received a letter from the Inland Revenue he became convinced he was behind in his taxes and that he faced utter disaster. To avoid his problems he killed himself by standing in front of a train. Even more tragically, far from being in arrears, Holt was owed 1,400 Australian dollars by the taxman.

Isecke Heinz *(suicide 1975)*

By November 1975 Heinz Isecke, a 56-year-old plumber, had been hiccupping forty times a minute for thirteen months. He was losing nearly 8 lb a month. Isecke tried countless cures that were proposed to him – including gargling with soapy water and swallowing gum – before he chose the ultimate solution. He jumped to his death from his second-floor hospital window.

Lester Edward *(suicide 1978)*

Edward Lester, aged thirty-one, was travelling alone by car along a road south of Katherine in Australia's Northern Territory when he crashed his car. The crash was by no means severe, and Lester was able to walk away. This indeed he did, and after walking a short distance across the countryside, he found a tree, arranged a rudimentary noose and hanged himself.

Liarsky Stephen *(suicide 1935)*

Like so many others, Stephen Liarsky, twenty-six, had failed to gain employment through the hard years of America's Depression. And like some of them he chose death rather than endless unemployment. His method, however, was out of the ordinary. Liarsky, of Worcester, Massashusetts, sent off to California for a mail order special: a black widow spider. He deliberately provoked the spider, whose bite is deadly, to attack him. When he was discovered and rushed to hospital the poison had already taken too great a hold for an antidote to be useful. The spider was found in a perforated cardboard box next to Liarsky's bed, with a couple of cards specifying the venom of its bite and the offer of another spider, plus its infant, for a five dollar investment. Meanwhile, in his hospital bed, Liarsky slowly suffocated as the poison formed a choking liquid that finally filled his lungs.

Liebaut Albert and Germaine *(suicide 1923)*

Newlyweds of just six days, the Liebauts were found dead – both shot – in a bedroom of their home at Suresnes near Paris. Germaine Liebaut had on her wedding dress and police worked out that the 22-year-old bride had first shot her thirty-year-old husband and then herself. A note addressed to the police announced this strange reason for their joint demise:

We are killing ourselves because we are too happy . . . we do not need money, for we are worth over 30,000 francs. We have good health and a wonderful future before us, but we prefer to die now because we are the happiest people in the world. We adore each other but would rather descend into the grave together while we are still so happy.

McClung Alexander *(suicide 1855)*

McClung was an early-nineteenth-century lawyer in Kentucky and Mississippi who came to be known as the Black Knight of the South because of his reputation as a deadly duellist. In 1855 he blew out his brains with his duelling pistol after pinning to his shirt-front a poem that he had written, entitled 'Ode To Death'. In the period

leading up to his death, he had grown increasingly
introspective and depressed, saying that, wherever he
went, at the end of each day he saw in the gathering dusk a
procession of grey men, the shades of all those whom he
had killed in his many duels.

Marcus Stewart and Cyril *(twin suicides 1975)*

The identical Marcus twins seemed to have the world in
their hands. Gynaecologists by training, their practice as
exclusive 'infertility specialists' soon brought them fame
and fortune. Yet, despite the surface success, the twins
seemd less and less able to deal with the real world. The
doorman in their luxury apartment house on East 63rd St,
New York City, found them too arrogant even to say 'good
morning'. Patients found them increasingly paranoid,
unable to restrain their irritation and even outright
insulting behaviour. Colleagues found them remote,
distant and icy. Gradually, as this remoteness increased,
the twins found their careers melting away. Colleagues
and patients alike would not tolerate their strange
behaviour. The grim truth came out in July 1975. For two
days their neighbours were complaining that an
unpleasant smell was coming from apartment 10H, the
Marcus's home. When janitor Bill Terrell went to check,
he recognised the smell that meant only one thing: a
corpse. He called the police. When the cops smashed their
way into the apartment the moist July air hit the
air-conditioned coolness of the apartment and a slight mist
moved over the scene. When it cleared they saw an
appalling sight: Stewart Marcus lay face up on the floor,
naked but for his socks. Cyril, in underpants only, lay face
down on the bed. Around them lay rotting food, laundry
wrappers, toilet articles, sweets, cakes, decaying take-away
dinners and mounds of human excrement. All in all it was
a carpet of garbage some eighteen inches deep which had
accumulated over more than a year. The story remained

bizarre even after the police and medical examiner had pieced it together. Unknown to their public, the Marcuses were barbiturate addicts. Gradually the semblance of normality that ruled their lives outside the apartment had fallen away. In July 1975 the balance tipped. Sometime between 10 and 14 July they had decided to end it all. They could no longer persist in their pretences and had decided on a mutual and final barbiturate overdose. Stewart duly died, but Cyril had developed a greater tolerance. He had passed out with his brother but some time later he must have woken up, groggy and confused, aware that his suicide had failed. In a final effort he had dressed himself and gone out on to the street one last time. Life without his twin must have seemed impossible. They had always been close, with that psychic kinship that is common between identical twins. Cyril had returned to the debris-strewn apartment, where the corpse of his brother was already decomposing, its face rotting away to such an extent that when the police found it they were unable to identify the differences between the twins. Cyril had no more pills so he took the tough way out: the cramps and convulsions of acute barbiturate withdrawal. But more than that, Cyril died because his brother had gone before him. He had no food, he had no will to live. Alone with decay he waited, willingly, for the end.

Mishima Yukio *(ritual suicide 1971)*

Mishima was Japan's leading literary figure when he killed himself, aged forty-five, in 1971. But literary fame was insufficient satisfaction for a man who was obsessed with the contemporary decline of his nation and whose worship of the flesh in the form of his own body-building became a personal religion. Mishima constantly called for a return to the old Japan, to the values and virtues of militarism. When these were not forthcoming from the microchip world, Mishima and an aide appeared in the office of an army general. Here he killed himself by ritual *seppuku* (more widely known as *hara kiri*). After he stabbed himself in the stomach, his aide slashed off the writer's head with one sweep of a razor-sharp sword.

Moon James *(suicide twentieth century)*

Suicide extraordinary, Moon constructed a Heath-Robinson-style device in his hotel room in Lafayette, Louisiana, to bring about his own death. Limitations of space prevent a complete description of his machine here, but basically it was a home-made guillotine with a delayed-action trigger based on a candle burning down to the point where it would burn through a rope. Underneath the blade was a specially made box on which Moon rested his head, having first strapped himself in position. The box was full of chloroform-soaked cotton, so that all Moon had to do was light the candle and lie back to await the anaesthesia that would precede his decapitation. The apparatus weighed over 50 kilograms. It worked.

Mora Jesus *(suicide twentieth century)*

A determined and highly individualistic Spanish suicide. Mora, a 31-year-old bachelor, had the unusual ambition of wishing to be eaten alive by lions. He did his best to achieve that end by repeatedly trying to enter the lions' enclosure in a safari park near Barcelona. Each time he was seized by security guards and handed over to the police; but the latter found that they had no reason to detain him. Eventually he succeeded in eluding the guards and climbed over the safety netting into an enclosure occupied by no fewer than forty lions. By the time the guards had driven off the lions, Mora had been torn to pieces.

Moyes Elizabeth *(suicide nineteenth century)*

Miss Moyes, the daughter of a baker, was unable to take the possible loss of status, money and class when her father lost his money. The last straw was when she was told to help support the family by taking up a position with a confectioners. So appalling was this drop in situation that she climbed the Monument in London's City and hurled herself 175 feet to a painful death on the pavement below.

Philaeni The *(voluntarily buried alive)*

The Philaeni were two brothers in ancient Carthage who resolved in a unique way a dispute with the neighbouring Cyrenaeans about land boundaries. It had been agreed that a disputed border should be decided by simultaneous expeditions from each city towards the other; the point at which the two parties met was to be the agreed boundary. However, the Philaeni, who formed the Carthaginian party, covered so much more ground than the Cyrenaeans that the latter accused them of cheating and said that they would accept the boundary only if the Philaeni would allow themselves to be buried alive on the spot in question. This the patriotic Philaeni did.

Pillsbury *(suicide)*

This young man of Chelsea, Massachusetts, killed himself with a complicated machine reminiscent of that used by the ingenious James Moon (above). He constructed a guillotine in his barn and attached to it a time-set trigger, worked by water running out of the holes in a bucket and so gradually reducing the leverage that held the blade in place. He then lay below the blade with his head over an open bottle of ether and slept away his last few minutes.

Redsall Peter *(suicide twentieth century)*

Car fanatic Redsall could not face the idea of his sporty Jaguar ever losing a race. Thus when another driver beat his vehicle, the thirty-year-old Englishman produced a pistol, wounded the other driver with three shots and then turned the gun fatally on himself.

Seneca Lucius Annaeus *(suicide 65 AD)*

The famous Stoic philosopher of ancient Rome proved almost as difficult to kill – even with his own active cooperation – as did the wild monk Rasputin centuries later. Sentenced to death by Nero, on the flimsiest of evidence that he had been involved in a plot against the Emperor's life, Seneca was given the opportunity of executing himself. This he attempted by cutting open the veins of his arms. But the circulatory problems of old age slowed the flow of blood. To hasten the end, Seneca therefore cut the veins in his ankles and behind his knees, meanwhile dictating a dissertation to his secretaries. At this point he asked his wife (who had voluntarily cut her own veins to die with him) to go to another bedroom. Still his death was slow coming. He persuaded his doctor to bring poison, which he drank, also to no effect. He was then placed in a bath of warm water, in the hope of hastening the action of either the bloodletting or the poison. Still he survived. Finally he was put in a steam bath, where he suffocated.

Stanton Louise Turck *(suicide 1933)*

Wealthy, attractive and youthful, Florida socialite Mrs Stanton had no reason to worry, until her husband died in a car crash. Devoted to his memory, she found life alone insupportable. Two weeks after his death she penned a brief note: 'I'm just going out into space to find out what it's all about; if there isn't anything that will be OK too.' She then borrowed on some pretext a friend's aeroplane, filled it with sufficient fuel for four hours' flying and took off, heading due east out over the Atlantic. Four hours later friends discovered her letter. Airmen were alerted and flew out after her, but neither the plane nor Mrs Stanton's body were ever found.

Stratton John *(suicide twentieth century)*

Stratton was depressed after his wife had left him. He decided on suicide by gas. He sealed doors and windows and turned on the gas oven, waiting patiently for the end. What he had forgotten was that his newly adapted supply of North Sea gas was non-toxic. The house filled with fumes but he remained unharmed. Thinking things over, Stratton decided that he might as well live. To celebrate he lit a cigar. North Sea gas may not be toxic, but it is still highly inflammable. Stratton and his house were blown to pieces.

Surgey *(suicide twentieth century)*

The death of an insurance clerk named Surgey is of special interest for the brilliant piece of medical detective work by which the famous forensic pathologist Sir Bernard Spilsbury reconstructed the victim's last moments. While walking home, Surgey cut his throat in the street with a pocket-knife that he then closed and put back in his coat pocket. He was found dead, with dilated pupils, holding a bloodstained handkerchief. From this evidence as well as from a trail of bloodstains along the footpath, Spilsbury was able to deduce that, after completely severing his jugular vein, Surgey had changed his mind about suicide and had attempted to stop the flow of blood with his handkerchief, at the same time walking towards the nearest doctor's house instead of towards his own. After turning a corner he had momentarily removed his handkerchief from the wound, thus letting air into his veins and causing death from air embolism. The pupils of his eyes had been dilated due to paralysis of the sympathetic nerves caused the pressure of the handkerchief on Surgey's neck.

Tapon Samuel *(suicide 1934)*

French millionaire Samuel Tapon left over £1.5 million at his death, but it was a relatively minor loss that brought this wealthy landowner to the point of self-destruction. A minor speculation failed and Tapon found himself some £50,000 out of pocket. So wretched did this loss make the miser that he determined on suicide. It was noted by the press that Tapon never betrayed his character even at the last. Walking into the local hardware shop to purchase the rope, he bargained on his purchase, managing to knock a few centimes off the price. Such a victory was obviously insufficient, for he returned to his home and hanged himself forthwith.

Tellegen Lou *(suicide 1934)*

Lou Tellegen started his career as a Dutch matinée idol. Drawn irresistibly to Hollywood, he starred in dozens of silent movies. His hits included *Single Wives*, *The Redeeming Sin* and similar melodramas of the 1920s. Now, with the silents overwhelmed by the talkies, Tellegen, like so many early stars, found his career over. By 1934 he was a nobody, and suicide must have seemed a welcome release. Alone in the dingy room that was now his home, Tellegen took out his many files of adulatory press clippings. He sorted through them, choosing all the best and every one that featured his one-time co-star and ex-wife Geraldine Farrar, and spread them in a great circle around the floor. Then he stripped himself naked and sat in the middle of the hundreds of faded tributes. He picked up the long, solid gold scissors that once he had used to cut out these very notices. Then he committed *hara kiri*, stabbing himself several times with the sharp pointed scissors. His body was found completely eviscerated, the heart exposed. The once yellowing notices were scarlet with Lou Tellegen's blood.

Vatel *(suicide nineteenth century)*

One Vatel, a French gourmet, was so overcome by his inability, as he felt, to prepare a sufficiently sumptuous meal for his fastidious friends that, rather than disappoint them, he killed himself.

Villeneuve N. *(suicide nineteenth century)*

One of Napoleon's admirals, Villeneuve committed suicide with businesslike efficiency. He had been in command of the French fleet at the Battle of Trafalgar and, after being imprisoned and then released by the British, he fell into disfavour with Napoleon. He killed himself by running a long pin into his heart; but first he bought a set of anatomical engravings, in order to acquaint himself thoroughly with the precise location of his target.

Kill or cure

Anonymous American male
(stabbed twentieth century)

The records of Dr Milton Helpern, former chief medical examiner to the city of New York, include the case of a man who was struck in the chest with an ice pick. He suffered only a small wound, from which he felt no ill effects, and did not bother consulting a doctor. For eight months he lived a normal life, and then he died. The autopsy showed that a piece from the tip of the ice pick, half a centimetre long, had broken off *inside* the man's heart.

Anonymous Australian
(buried in manure twentieth century)

A young boy in Victoria, Australia, was killed some years ago by the well-meant ministrations of a practitioner of folk medicine. The latter buried the boy up to his neck in a pile of manure for long periods at a time, and the intense heat generated within the manure fatally raised the boy's body temperature.

Anonymous Dane *(accidental death 1978)*

A Danish man, aged twenty-six, went into hospital for what should have been simple enough operation for intestinal blockage. Unfortunately for him, surgeons were using electrically heated knives to perform the operation.

One of these knives burnt through the patient's digestive tract and ignited the explosive gases in his stomach. The resultant explosion was so violent that it destroyed parts of his colon. Surgical efforts failed to repair the damage and the victim died of blood poisoning shortly afterwards.

Anonymous German murderer
(dissected alive eighteenth century)

According to the *Newgate Calendar*, a particularly vicious German murderer of the eighteenth century was about to be dissected, after his execution by hanging, when the surgeon noticed that he was still alive. After drawing this to the attention of the other surgeons present, he reminded them of the nature of the man's crime and calmly announced that it seemed best to proceed with the dissection, which he did.

Anonymous male *(dissected alive 1587)*

According to Stow's *Annals*, a man who had been hanged in London in 1587 was taken to the 'chirurgeons' Hall . . . to have made of him an anatomie'. When the surgeon cut open his chest, he discovered that the heart was still beating. Evidently the man had been only half-strangled by the hangman's rope. The chest wound, however, proved fatal.

Anonymous woman *(poisoned in error)*

A young Wiltshire woman dispensed indigestion powders for the patients of a local doctor. On one occasion, a patient complained about his new bottle of indigestion powder which, he said, made him feel terrible. The young woman was rather sensitive to criticism and reacted by taking a large dose of the powder herself to prove there was nothing wrong with it. She died within twenty-four hours. The wholesalers had inadvertently sent her a batch of sodium fluoride instead of indigestion powder.

Anonymous woman
(killed by surgical error twentieth century)

In the Helpern records is the case of a 35-year-old woman who suffered severe cramps after an appendectomy and was opened up a second time. It was found that the first surgeon had left a surgical clamp inside her abdomen. The second surgeon removed the clamp and repaired the internal damage it had caused. The patient subsequently died. The second surgeon had left a surgical gauze pad inside her abdomen.

B.F. *(internal injuries twentieth century)*

B.F. are the initials of a 55-year-old woman who died in hospital as a result of a freak accident while she was being prepared for an ear operation. She had been anaesthetised and was being given oxygen when an explosion occurred, hurling the anaesthetist to the floor and starting a fire on his trolley. At first the patient did not seem to have been hurt and the operation continued. Shortly afterwards, however, she died. The post-mortem revealed internal injuries, from which it was concluded the explosion had taken place inside the mouthpiece with which she was being given oxygen, and that there had possibly been another explosion inside her stomach. A spark caused by static electricity was thought to have ignited the oxygen.

Bentham Jeremy *(embalmed 1832)*

Bentham, the 'Father of Utilitarianism', died at the age of eighty-four in London. He willed his entire estate to University College, London, on condition that his body be preserved and placed in attendance at all of the College Hospital's board meetings. One Dr Southward Smith was to prepare his corpse. Once Bentham was dead, Smith reconstructed the skeleton and placed a wax impression of the philosopher's head on top. He then dressed the body in suitable clothes and a hat. The whole creation was then enclosed in a mahogany case, with folding glass doors. His favourite walking stick placed in one hand, the philosopher thus began what turned out to be ninety-two years of boardroom observation.

Bibby John *(died of malnutrition 1939)*

Seventeen-year-old John Bibby, mute since birth, had depended utterly on his mother's incomparable care and devotion throughout his short life. Among other problems, John was never capable of chewing his own food, and, like a mother bird for her fledglings, Mrs Emily Bibby had always chewed up his portion before feeding it to her son. When, inevitably, his mother fell ill, John Bibby was rushed to hospital to be looked after. Without the power of speech, the young man was unable to explain how he ate; when he did, for the first time, attempt to chew his own food, the effort proved fatal. A coroner's jury reported death by misadventure on Bibby, who choked to death when attempting an otherwise simple human activity.

Biggers Jack *(died of apoplexy eighteenth century)*

Biggers was a British glutton whose enormous appetite finally laid him low. Inside one hour he devoured six pounds of bacon, a dozen suet dumplings, a vast green salad, a loaf of bread and a gallon of beer. He then suffered a fatal bout of apoplexy.

Bishop Washington Irving
(?killed by premature autopsy 1899)

This New York magician was subject to cataleptic attacks, and always carried a letter warning of his condition and forbidding autopsy in the event of apparent death. On one occasion he was actually pronounced dead by two doctors but revived twelve hours later. On 12 May 1899 Bishop collapsed onstage during a performance and lapsed into a coma. He was pronounced dead the next day and, despite his letter of warning, an autopsy was carried out. No physical cause of death could be found. It is thus possible that the autopsy itself killed him.

Burke Pat and **O'Rourke** Billy
(scrubbed to death 1903)

Both these American tramps suffered death from cleanliness. In August 1903 they were taken into a hostel in St Louis and given their first bath in twenty years. Whether or not it was the protective accumulation of dirt being so suddenly removed that killed them we do not know. It may have been the fact that both men were scrubbed with a broom.

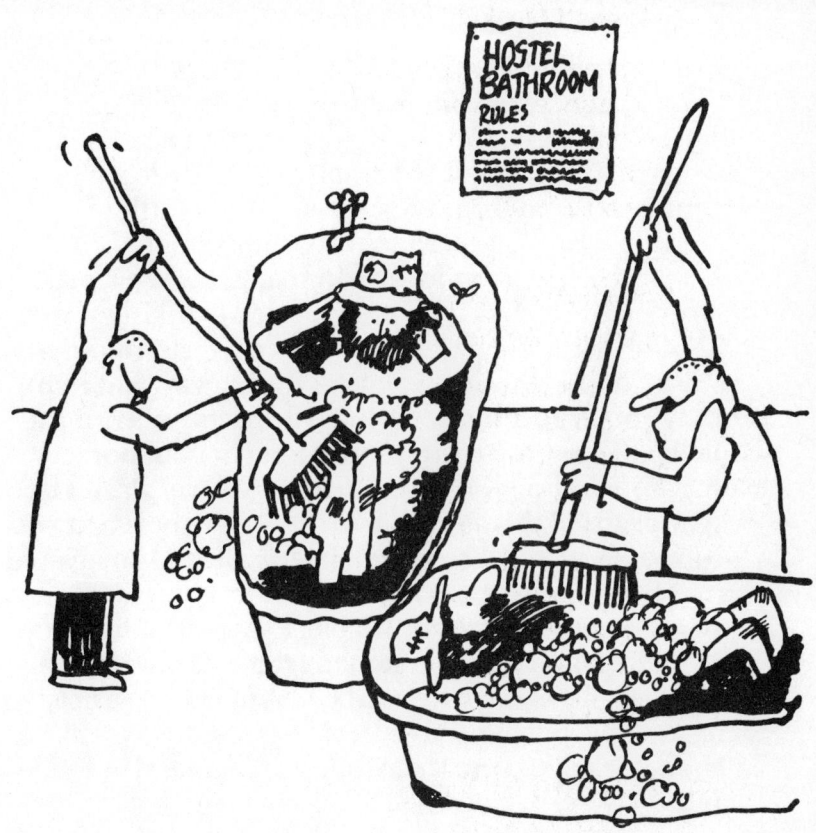

Burke William *(hanged and dissected 1830)*

One half of the infamous bodysnatching team Burke and Hare was dissected after death, just as his victims had been. His skin was cut up and made into tobacco pouches and wallets.

Burns Robert *(1796)*

From 1795, when his only daughter died, Scotland's
greatest poet entered on the long and painful decline that
ended in his death. Shocked and grief-stricken, he
contracted a bad case of rheumatic fever. He lost his
appetite, suffered trembling fits and found little sleep in
nights dominated by terrible and continuous pain. On his
doctor's advice Burns moved to a spa, Brow Well, on the
Solway Firth. Here his regime included drinking several
pints of iron water every day, followed by lengthy walks
out into the cold muddy waters of the Solway, where Burns
would submerge himself up to his armpits for as long as he
could bear. His days ended with a long bout of horse
riding, concluding with a nightcap of several glasses of
port. Months of this alleged cure proved to be having quite
the opposite effect. The poet was so weak and emaciated
that he had to be helped out of his chair. His wasted
features were barely recognisable. His rheumatic fever
returned, savaging his weakened frame. He went home,
exhausted and barely alive, to be troubled by a variety of
petty debts. He collapsed on arrival into a box bed in his
kitchen. He never rose from that resting place, but died
four days later.

Eglantina Dr *(stung to death 1975)*

The African honey-bee has a tough life. There is little
pollen or nectar in its native habitat and there are many
animals who will happily destroy the hive. Thus the bee
has grown far more aggressive than its European
counterpart. It is, on the other hand, a far superior
producer of honey. In 1956 geneticist Walter E. Kerr,
working in Rio Claro, Brazil, tried to breed a superbee by
combining strains of African and European bees. He
imported forty-seven African queens and set to work. In
1957 a visiting beekeeper accidentally released some

twenty-six colonies into the neighbouring jungle. In the wild the bees developed, their tough African strain staying predominant. Since 1957 the new superbee, known generally as the Brazilian killer bee, has been moving through South America at the rate of 200 miles per year. These bees are truly deadly. One of their victims was Brazilian schoolteacher Dr Eglantina. Through pure ill luck the teacher managed to disturb the hypersensitive bees. Hundreds and thousands swarmed at her, covering her head and her body. She tried to run away but a lame leg and the bees' tenacity made this impossible – the swarming bees pumped their venom imto her. Experiments have shown that these bees can sting more than 500 times in a brief sixty seconds. The human body simply cannot tolerate that intensive a level of poisoning. As Dr Eglantina struggled, people rushed towards her to help but they too were driven off. Firemen arrived, but were helpless until they brought smoking torches and drove the bees off. Dr Eglantina was rushed to hospital but it was too late. Thousands of stings had torn her flesh and poisoned her body.

Long St John *(died of consumption nineteenth century)*

An early-nineteenth-century quack, Long's speciality was a secret mixture that he claimed was an infallible cure for consumption. He himself died at the early age of thirty-six of – you guessed it – consumption.

May Thomas *(choked 1650)*

This portly English historian found that as his double chins multiplied the best way of supporting them was with successive strips of cloth tied tightly round them. Unfortunately as the chins grew the cloths tightened and finally choked him.

Pascal Blaise *(poisoned by his doctors 1662)*

The great seventeenth-century scientist and man of letters seems to have been killed at the age of thirty-nine by the well-meant ministrations of his own doctors. He suffered from ill health throughout his life, and there is evidence that the nature and quality of the medicines pressed upon him by his doctors were such that they brought about his death by poisoning.

Pass Mr *(died of fright 1803)*

The beadle of the Company of Surgeons in 1803 died of fright at what he saw in the rooms of Professor Aldini. The latter, according to the *Newgate Calendar*, had been carrying out electrical experiments upon the corpse of a criminal named George Foster, who had recently been hanged at the Old Bailey. Aldini managed to galvanise some of the muscles of the presumably dead Foster into action so that the jaw quivered, an eye opened, the right hand moved and clenched the fist and both legs moved also. Mr Pass was among a number of observers, many of whom were terrified at the spectacle of Foster apparently being resurrected from the dead. This led to quite a commotion among the general public and it was widely believed at the time that Foster had been killed not on the scaffold but on Professor Aldini's table.

Pontico Baby Ruth *(choked 1942)*

This was a tragic case of death being caused, in what would normally be a harmless situation, by the special problems of a freakish physique *(see* also Merrick, John, page 77).Baby Ruth Pontico was a famous circus fat lady, who at her heaviest had a mass of 370 kilograms (816 lb). In 1942, she checked into a Florida hospital for what should have been a relatively minor operation to remove tumours from her knees. The operation was a success, but as Ruth came out of anaesthesia she started to vomit. In such cases the patient is turned on his/her side to prevent choking. But she was simply too heavy, a problem that had not been considered in advance. The nurses struggled desperately to turn her over, but with her immense weight she was immovable, and she choked to death.

Power Frederick *(electrocuted twentieth century)*

Mr Power, of Newcastle, Australia, hated cats and set up a trap for them in his backyard. The trap consisted of a small sardine can containing meat, connected to an electrical cable which he plugged into his garage power point. The aptly-named Power was found lying face down in the yard with his hands round the sardine can. The coroner was unable to establish how he had come to make contact with the live can. It is worth noting, perhaps, that cats in laboratory experiments have learned to manipulate switches successfully.

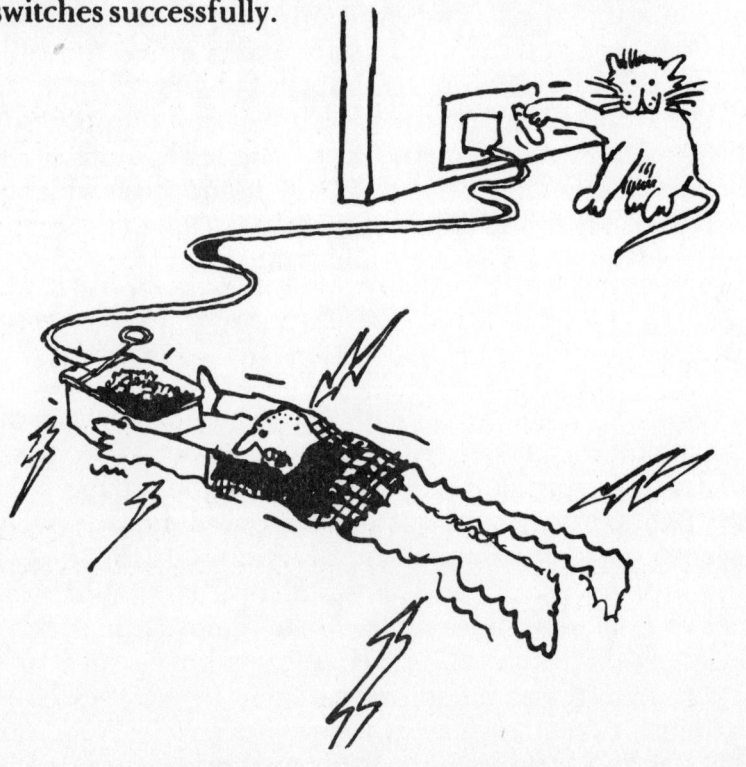

Prevost D'Exiles Antoine-François

(killed by medical error 1763)

This eighteenth-century French writer, the author of 170 volumes including the famous *Manon Lescaut,* suffered a stroke in 1763 and was found apparently lifeless. An ignorant magistrate ordered an equally ignorant surgeon to open the body to look for the cause of death. The surgeon began by making a deep incision down the chest and abdomen, whereupon the victim screamed loudly and opened his eyes, only to die from the effects of the incision.

Rieu Madame Paul *(poisoned 1951)*

Madame Rieu was one of the four citizens of the French village of Pont St Esprit who died in August 1951 in a famous case of mass poisoning by ergot that had accidentally contaminated a particular day's supply of bread. More than two hundred villagers were poisoned by a disease that was known to their medieval forbears as 'St Anthony's fire'; thirty of them were driven quite insane. They saw terrifying hallucinations and behaved as though possessed by devils. Madame Rieu failed in an attempt at suicide, but died anyway. An eleven-year-old boy named Charles Graugeon tried to strangle his own mother. Marthe Toulouse tried to throw herself into the River Rhône to quench the fiery serpents she believed were consuming her. Someone fired his gun at an imaginary monster he thought he saw chasing him. When the villagers who had been driven mad were taken to lunatic asylums their behaviour was such that it terrified even the existing inmates.

Simon Beth Ann *(died of acute malnutrition 1965)*

Beth Ann Simon and her husband were early hippies.
Ostensibly artists, they were devoted to drugs, mysticism,
arcane diets and the full range of the 'alternative' lifestyle.
Beth Ann turned to the work of self-styled
philosopher-scientist George Osawa. In his work *Zen
Macrobiotics* she found what she hoped would be the cure
for her problems, in particular a vicious and recurrent
migraine. The cure was diet No. 7, a very simple diet of tea
and a little grain which she was allowed to vary with a
macrobiotic staple 'gomasio', or sesame seeds and sea salt.
The diet rated perilously low on vitamins, calcium and
other nutritients but, with its regimen of chewing every
mouthful fifty times, it promised success 'through the
absolute justice and infinite wisdom of the order of the
universe'. Sure enough, after a month of No. 7, Beth Ann
and her husband, who had joined in, had lost 9 kg (20 lb).
But as Beth Ann grew more and more enmeshed in the
world of Zen macrobiotics, the diet started to have less
positive effects. She lost more weight, her back and hips
started to hurt, her legs swelled and she came out in boils.
The remedy for these disorders was a daily third of a pint
of radish juice for three days. It didn't help Beth Ann. She
turned to the head of the Osawa Foundation, Irma Paule.
Paule advised raw vegetables; she didn't mention to Beth
Ann that what she needed was a cure for her real
problems: scurvy and anorexia nervosa (obsessive fasting).
The vegetables didn't help, and by now Beth Ann was
convinced that more rather than less rigour was needed.
She fasted for some fourteen days in September 1965 and
it seemed to help her aches and pains. Her weight,
however, was a meagre 36.3 kg (80 lb). She was literally
skin and bones, and the whites of her sunken eyes could be
seen underneath the irises. Beth Ann was dying, but she
wrote to Osawa, who replied: 'You are a brave girl, stay on
diet No. 7.' In the meantime, Charlie Simon started

reading up on the diet. He found another Osawa book which stressed that diet No. 7 should be used for a maximum of two months. Beth Ann had gone far beyond that limit. She wrote again to the guru. His letter arrived on 9 November – completely contradictory to his previous one. Osawa said simply that far from being 'brave' Beth Ann had misunderstood the diet and should start over again. By this time his advice was irrelevant. On the morning of 9 November, Charlie was feeding Beth Ann the only dish she could manage – puréed carrots. She smiled up at him and said, 'That's good', then her eyes rolled up, her head slumped in his hands and she died. When the police arrived thirty minutes later, Charlie was still desperately giving his wife mouth-to-mouth resuscitation.

Slotkin Louis *(died of radiation 1946)*

As he worked in his laboratory on 21 May 1946, nuclear physicist Louis Slotkin blundered. His hand slipped and he permitted two masses of uranium to approach each other too closely. The result was a blinding flash, at which point Slotkin and his colleagues were drenched with lethal radiation. Although the end results of such immolation in radiation are initially agonising and in due course fatal, the sufferer is unimpaired at first. With this in mind Slotkin coolly calculated the dosage of radiation that every member of the team had received. After a short while he was able to announce that he alone had absorbed so much radiation that he must die. He then said goodbye to his colleagues, assured them they would survive and left the laboratory for a nearby hospital. Nine days later, as he had estimated, Louis Slotkin was dead.

Vaudille *(bled to death nineteenth century)*

Vaudille was a French miser who carried the principle of parsimony too far for his own good. In accordance with medical practices of the day, he was to be bled for health reasons; and he sought in advance to obtain this service for the best possible price. The barber-surgeon who was to perform the operation told him that the bleeding would need to be done on three separate occasions over a period of time, at a charge of three *sous* for each bleeding, totalling nine *sous* in all. Vaudille, however, insisted that the full amount of blood should be withdrawn at one bleeding, thus enabling him to pay only once and thereby save six *sous*. The barber-surgeon obliged, and the loss of blood proved too much for Vaudille, who went into shock and died.

Whipple Wayne *(died of obesity 1978)*

Farmboy Wayne Whipple, aged twenty-six, was a solid 108 kg (17 stone) when in 1974 a hay elevator fell on him. While Wayne survived the accident, something utterly disastrous happened to his glands. From being simply a big muscular man, Wayne started to turn into a ballooning monster. Doctors tried in vain to discover the cause of his mounting growth, as Wayne's body defied all medical knowledge and grew and grew. Diets were useless and the fat continued to swell. By 1978 his waistline measured an astounding 173 cm (68 in). He was unable to walk more than fifty steps without stopping to get his breath. He slept sixteen hours every day. Weighing in at a massive 320 kg (50 stone) meant there wasn't a clothing store that could accommodate his giant body. He was reduced to sewing two pairs of trousers together for some makeshift covering. Finally he was forced to spend all his time in bed. Wayne Whipple met his inevitable end, dying of a heart attack when his body gave up trying to service the mountain of fat.

Woulfe Peter *(died of pneumonia 1805)*

An eminent chemist and Fellow of the Royal Society, Woulfe died in 1805 as a direct result of treating himself once too often with his own extraordinary all-purpose illness remedy. Whenever he fell sick, his practice was to take a non-stop coach journey to Edinburgh and back to London. This remarkable cure for disease served him well until his final expedition, in the course of which a cold developed into pneumonia, to which he succumbed.

To a place of execution

Anaxarchus *(pounded to death c. 340 BC)*

This unfortunate philosopher, who was a member of
Alexander the Great's entourage, foolishly offended the
king of Cyprus. For his insolence he was pounded to death
in a large stone mortar.

Arethusa Marcus, Bishop of
(stung to death first century)

The bishop suffered like many fellow-Christians under the persecutions of the Roman Emperors. He was hung up in a basket, smeared with honey and stung to death by voracious wasps.

Beane Sawney (Sandy) and his family
(mutilated and burnt alive 1435)

Sawney Beane and his eight sons, six daughters, eighteen grandsons and fourteen granddaughters – every one the product of an incestuous union within the tribe – were a band of savage, murderous and cannibalistic Scottish bandits who preyed on travellers along the bleak west coast of Scotland in the fifteenth century. Safe in their headquarters – a tortuous cave system in which piles of loot strewed the floor and expertly butchered smoked and salted human carcasses hung like hams from the ceiling – the Beanes carried on a reign of terror until 1435, when King James IV himself led the posse that managed to capture the terrible clan. All forty-seven Beanes were summarily tried at Leith. Not surprisingly they were all found guilty. As the females watched, first the penises and then the hands and feet of the males were slashed off. They were then left to bleed to death where they lay. The women were thrown alive into three great fires, where they swiftly and painfully expired.

Blandina *(tortured to death c. 170AD)*

Eusebius's account of the death of Blandina, who was one of the early Christian martyrs during the reign of Marcus Aurelius, serves to give some idea of what it was like to be executed at a Roman circus as a spectacle for the mob. First Blandina was compelled to watch some of her friends die in the arena. Next she was forced to run between two lines of armed men who struck her with their whips and iron bars. After this she was hung from a high pole as bait for a group of ravenous hyenas and wolves. Before they could actually get at her, she was cut down and made to watch her younger brother being flogged, roasted over a fire and finally thrown to the animals to eat. Eventually she was wrapped in a net and hung from a beam at the edge of the arena, where wild bulls charged her and gored her to death as she swung back and forth.

The Earl of Carlisle *(hanged, drawn and quartered 1315)*

The award of the Court is that for your treason you will be drawn, hanged and beheaded; that your heart and bowels and entrails, whence came your traitorous thoughts, be torn out and burnt to ashes and that the ashes be scattered to the winds; that your body be cut into four quarters, and that one of them be hanged upon the tower of Carlisle, another upon the tower of Newcastle, a third upon the bridge of York and the fourth at Shrewsbury, and that your head be set upon London Bridge.

Corday Charlotte *(guillotined)*

When the killer of Marat was executed by guillotine, her head bounced off the platform and was seized by an executioner's assistant named Legros. He struck the head a blow in the face, whereupon, to the astonishment of those nearby, the whole face reacted in anger, as though Corday were still alive and conscious.

Corder William *(hanged 1828)*

Corder was the killer of Maria Marten in the famous 'Red Barn' murder of 1827. After Corder's execution in August 1828, his body was dissected by medical students; this had actually been a requirement under the death sentence as pronounced by the judge. Prison officials then presented

J. Curtis of the London *Times*, who had covered the murder and trial for his paper, with a piece of Corder's skin big enough to use for binding a copy of his account of the affair.

Cortachy Castle Drummer of
(hurled from battlements)

A handsome young drummer, whose name has not been recorded, was caught in *flagrante delicto* with the lady of the castle. As punishment he was sealed within his own drum, then carried in silence to the top of the highest tower and thrown down.

Cory *(crushed to death seventeenth century)*

This poor man was executed as a witch at Salem during the great seventeenth-century witch scare in New England. He was one of the few courageous enough not to plead guilty under torture, and he was therefore condemned to death by pressing – *peine forte et dure* – a form of execution in which the victim was spreadeagled with his body beneath a board, on to which heavier and heavier rocks were placed until the ribs were cracked, the intestines burst and the lungs crushed. Cory's execution by this barbaric process was the occasion for a strange act of gratuitous brutality. As Cory was *in extremis*, his tongue involuntary protruded from his mouth as an effect of the slow suffocation he was undergoing; whereupon the sheriff, standing over his head, forced it back into his mouth again with a cane.

Cosmas and **Damian** Saints

(multiple executions first century)

These two early Christian martyrs had to be executed five times before they would stay dead. They were unsuccessfully drowned, crucified, stoned and burnt before being successfully beheaded. Overkill?

Damiens Robert *(tortured to death 1757)*

Robert Damiens, or Robert the Devil as his contemporaries nicknamed him, tried unsuccessfully to assassinate King Louis XV of France. Neither his failure nor the apparent rationalism of the era persuaded the French authorities to relax the severity of their punishment for such *lèse-majesté*. First Damiens was tortured by being chained down to a steel bed which was heated over red-hot coals. Then, his body already lacerated and burnt, he was put on public display for his actual death. The hand that had struck the impotent blow was burned off and a mixture of boiling oil, molten lead, scalded pitch was used to cauterise the wound. Generally slashed about, Damiens was then attached to four horses, one wrenching at each of his limbs. The carters whipped up their steeds, but, strain as they might, the ropes merely tore at Damiens' flesh. The limbs stubbornly refused to separate from the agonised body. Only when a surgeon appeared and cut open the joints with a sharp knife did the horses manage to tear the would-be assassin into four bloody quarters. His remains were burnt and the ashes dispersed in the air.

Davis John *(hanged eighteenth century)*

An eighteenth-century malefactor who nearly got away with it: condemned to death on the gallows, Davis showed every sign of complete mental and physical collapse over the days leading up to his execution. He 'affected the most pitiful looks and deadly sickness imaginable' (to quote James Guthrie, Ordinary of Newgate) and had to be carried on the backs of others wherever he went. He vomited frequently in the prison chapel and seemed so thoroughly sick and wretched that his irons were knocked off and he was left untied while waiting in the cart beneath Tyburn Tree to be hanged. He lay completely prostrate in the cart while prayers were being said. Then, as Guthrie wrote:

as I was beginning to sing the seventh verse of the sixteenth Psalm, he . . . put his foot to the side of the cart, took hold of a spoke with his hand, and jumped over among the crowd in the twinkling of an eye. The officers and spectators were all of them surprised and astonished, and, some of the people favouring his escape, he ran very fast till he got over a field.

Alas, after all this effort he was caught and brought back to meet his fate. This time, the hangman did not wait for Guthrie to finish the psalm.

Djao 'Old Mother' *(death by a thousand cuts 1924)*

Old Mother Djao reigned as the most fearsome bandit in China's Santung Province. Forty-seven-year-old Djao, an expert horsewoman and ruthless in the exploitation of all around her, led a large band of outlaws. Among her unsavoury exploits was the wholesale massacre of sixty villagers – men, women, children, cattle and pets – who dared oppose her in a raid. Her demise came when a 'home guard', the 'Big Knife Society' of the town of Ichowfu, roundly defeated Djao and her followers. She was executed by the *ling-che* method, literally 'slicing' and generally known as 'the death of a thousand cuts'. *Ling-che* is, in fact, human vivisection, performed slowly with such skill that the victim survives in excruciating agony through hours of a hideous death.

Dun Thomas *(executed c.1120)*

Dun was a nototious bandit of the era of Henry I. Born in Bedfordshire, he had apparently gained a bad reputation as a child and his subsequent career did little to redeem it. He ran a skilful gang of pickpockets, strong-box breakers and the like, who added deft robberies to their more violent attacks. But the continuous terror which he wielded over rich and poor led to his downfall. Half the county joined in pursuing him, and despite efforts that would have graced a Hollywood melodrama, as he rode, swam, hid and fought to keep himself free, he was at last captured. When the wounds received in his capture had healed, he was given a most summary trial in Bedford marketplace and found guilty without any defence even being called. He was sentenced to death. When the two executioners came to carry out the sentence, Dun warned them not to touch him, and allegedly tossed them both to the ground nine times before they subdued him. Once they had secured him, the authorities took their dreadful revenge. First Dun's hands were chopped off at the wrist; then his arms at the elbows, then at about an inch below the shoulders. His legs were similarly treated, amputations being made first at the ankle, then the knee and finally high on the thighs. Finally his head was hacked from his still-living torso. The severed limbs were nailed to prominent parts of Bedford, while the head was burnt to ashes.

Edwards Edgar *(hanged 1902)*

Edgar Edwards uttered one of the most extraordinary last remarks ever. The murderer of John and Beatrice Darby in December 1902, Edwards was condemned to be hanged, despite pleas based on evidence that insanity ran in his family. That there was some truth in these pleas became evident when Edwards, on his way to the scaffold, remarked pleasantly to the chaplain: 'I've been looking forward to this.'

Elsom Eleanor *(tortured 1722)*

Elsom, who had murdered her husband, had been
condemned to the stake. Before leaving the prison she was
given a garment soaked in tar and all her limbs were
smeared with the same flammable substance; on her head
was put a bonnet also covered in tar. When she had been
driven through the streets of Lincoln to the place of
execution, she was placed on a tar barrel about three feet
high, on top of which the stake was fixed. Her body was
held fast to the stake by three iron bands, and she helped
the executioner fit a rope around her neck to press her
even closer. This rope was used to strangle her before the
flames actually reached her flesh, though once the fiercely
burning tar was lit there was no way of checking.

Ferrers Earl Lawrence *(hanged 1760)*

Earl Ferrers, the only nobleman to be hanged at Tyburn
like a commoner, rather than receive the more customary
decapitation that was the lot of the aristocracy, was a very
ordinary murderer. He killed his steward in a fit of
madness. Indeed, later courts might have declared him
unfit to plead, but in 1760 his crime took him to the
gallows. Still, as a nobleman, Ferrers retained certain
privileges, all of which he indulged. The usual prison cart
was replaced by a magnificent cortège that took three
hours to travel from the Tower to Tyburn. Two sheriffs, a
high constable, two parties of Grenadier Guards, both
mounted and on foot, not to mention the hearse that
would carry Earl Ferrers's corpse to his grave, all
accompanied his lordship to his death. The earl himself,
resplendent in a white satin wedding suit, stood on a
special platform with a rope around his neck. A black silk
rope had been ordered for the hanging, but there hadn't
been enough time to make it; the usual hemp was used.
The earl prayed, kneeling on black silk cushions, his arms

bound with a black silk sash. The only sour note came at the moment of hanging. After blessing the crowd and bestowing various gifts, Earl Ferrers stood peacefully awaiting his death. The hangman, Thomas Turlis, activated the drop, but it malfunctioned. With Turlis pulling on his legs, it took Earl Ferrers four agonising minutes to die.

Fish Albert *(electrocuted 1936)*

American child killer Albert Fish ranks as an inmate in anyone's chamber of horrors. Fish's twenty years of crime centred on his molesting and often killing about four hundred children. Those whom he killed he also dismembered, cooked and ate. From the age of five his life was one of unparalleled sexual perversity. A woman teacher developed in him a taste for being spanked on his bare flesh. He was obsessed with excreta and his anus. He would forces pieces of alcohol-soaked cotton into his rectum, then set fire to them. He also did this to many of his young victims. He was also wont to stick needles into himself around the scrotum, and a post-mortem found twenty-seven needles, often eroded into small pieces, embedded in his flesh. Many of the boys he attacked he castrated. This, like the rest of his sadism, came from his religious mania. He felt that God was driving him to further and further excess. The children were offered as sacrifices, to purge his own sins. In 1934 Fish was arrested for the murder of twelve-year-old Grace Budd, a girl whom he abducted, killed, raped, cooked and ate. Although Fish was patently insane, a horrified jury passed a death sentence on him. As it happened this delighted the killer. Like Peter Kurten, whose devout hope was that as the guillotine fell he would hear the sound of his own blood dripping into the basket, Fish embraced his execution. 'What a thrill it will be to die in the electric chair,' enthused the 66-year-old killer. 'The supreme thrill, the only one I haven't tried.' In the death chamber Fish rushed unaided to the chair and helped fix the electrodes himself. When the first massive jolt hit him, the current was short-circuited by all the metal embedded in his body. Instead of killing Fish instantly it created a blue haze that danced around his head and left him unharmed. A further massive jolt overrode the short circuit and Albert Fish, one of the world's vilest killers, was dead.

Fitzgerald 'Fighting' *(hanged eighteenth century)*

This infamous eighteenth-century brawler, cheat and killer known as 'Fighting' Fitzgerald met a most appropriate end. He had fought twenty or more duels, in the course of which he had killed or wounded most of his opponents without himself being hurt. He owed this record of success in conflict more to his unscrupulousness than to any great skill with weapons. He did not hesitate to fire his pistol out of turn and then claim it had gone off accidentally. Once he was caught wearing a concealed coat of armour underneath his normal clothes in a duel being fought with swords. Eventually convicted of murder and sentenced to be executed, he was hanged three times before he died. On each of the first two attempts the rope broke, causing Fitzgerald to have a severe attack of hysteria.

Geisslerin Clara *(tortured sixteenth century)*

A 69-year-old widow of Gelnhausen, in Germany, Geisslerin was denounced as a witch and tortured to death over a long period. First she was subjected to the thumbscrew, then her legs and feet were crushed to a pulp in iron vices. After this she was repeatedly stretched on the rack for several hours at a time, and this continued for days until she simply fell dead as she was being lifted off it.

The judicial authorities than pronounced that she had been invisibly strangled by the Devil so that she would not reveal his secrets.

Goodale Robert *(hanged 1885)*

Goodale was accidentally decapitated while being hanged at Norwich Castle on 30 November 1885 for the murder of his wife. He was a heavily built man, and the hangman miscalculated the length of the drop, with the result that the jerk at the end of Goodale's fall completely severed his head from his body.

Gourdon Bertrand de *(flayed alive 1199)*

Gourdon was the archer who fatally wounded Richard the Lionheart at the siege of Chalons Castle in 1199. Richard, aware that he was dying, gave Gourdon a full pardon and indeed a monetary reward, and ordered that he should be set free. But as soon as Richard was dead, Gourdon was seized and flayed alive.

Hamby Gordon Fawcett *(executed 1920)*

Stick-up man Hamby faced execution in Sing Sing's electric chair as a price for killing several bank clerks in an unsuccessful raid. With estimable sang-froid Hamby showed not a sign of fear and conducted himself enviably as his end approached. After sleeping a sound ten hours he wrote three last letters – to a girl and to each of his parents. Dressed in the obligatory black 'death suit' and dark shirt he managed to persuade the warden to let him have a white shirt, although a further request for a gaudy tie and stiff collar was turned down. Hamby breakfasted heartily, put away steak, mushrooms, strawberries and coffee for lunch and ordered a lobster salad for supper, joking with his guards that 'At least I'll not need to worry about indigestion.' A fellow inmate of the death house, hold-up man Frank Flanagan, obtained permission to treat his departing colleague and sent him cigars, bonbons and ice cream – all of which supplies were bequeathed to Hamby's surviving twenty-nine death row inmates. As he tucked into the lobster he urged everyone around to 'Smile, please, smile' and suggested that one miserable guard should be swapped for a cheerier fellow. He refused a benediction from the chaplain but stood in front of the chair smoking his last cigarette. Given permission to make a farewell statement, he informed those who watched:

I want to thank you for the wonderful treatment I have received here. You have been very kind to me . . . I don't wish to appear in the light of a moralist, but you can tell all young men from me not to ever start doing wrong, for once you start a career of crime you can never stop.

At which point he ground out his cigarette on the floor, seated himself calmly in the chair, and very soon afterwards the lights dimmed momentarily all through Sing Sing.

Hayes Catherine *(burnt at the stake 1726)*

Mrs Hayes was a particularly brutal killer who had done away with her husband. She had smashed his skull, dismembered his body, then deposited various pieces around London. Despite her plans, the pieces were not only found, but reassembled and traced back to her. The evidence was damning and Catherine Hayes was sentenced to death. Where she was particularly unfortunate was that in the eighteenth century the murder of a husband was accorded special legal status: the crime was known as 'petty treason'; the killing of the head of the family being, in miniature, the killing of a head of state. And for 'petty treason' there was but one penalty: burning alive at the stake. The law, dating from an even more barbarous age, had been modified by a recent law of George I – the executioner now strangled his victim before lighting the merely symbolic fire – but the penalty stood. When Hayes was tied to the stake and the faggots were piled around her legs, the executioner committed a monstrous error. Instead of waiting until he had done his job of strangling the woman, he lit the fire first. By the time he came to use his rope, the heat and flames were too intense. He had to stand back as the flames took hold on Hayes's flesh. As a vast crowd watched, the murderess, according to the letter of the law, was slowly and agonisingly roasted to death.

Hussein Brigadier *(beheaded 1971)*

Ugandan Army chief of staff at the time of General Amin's *coup* in January 1971, Hussein was one of the first to be killed under the new regime. According to a guard who was working for Amin at the time, Hussein's severed head was brought to Amin's house, where the general placed it on a table in front of him and made a speech to it, before placing it in his refrigerator.

Kemmler William *(electrocuted 1890)*

Kemmler had the dubious distinction of being the first person to die in the electric chair. The new method of execution was introduced in New York State in August 1890, despite considerable opposition from the inventor George Westinghouse, who had developed the high-tension AC system needed to operate the chair and who held the patents on the necessary equipment. Westinghouse was currently trying to win the mass market for his AC system and was concerned that publicity about the fatal effects of electrocution would frighten people off. Edison, on the other hand, held the patents for the much safer low-tension DC system and did everything he could to encourage the introduction of the electric chair. Kemmler's execution was badly botched. After receiving a 1,300 volt charge for seventeen seconds, he was found to be gasping for breath but still alive. The executioner then retightened the electrode on Kemmler's shaven head and gave him a full minute's charge. When doctors inspected his dead body it was too hot to touch.

Lacenaire Pierre François *(guillotined 1835)*

Pierre Lacenaire was both intellectual and criminal, a poet and essayist turned petty thief. While he stole more for social reasons than for gain, it was doubtless his failure to make a name as a scribbler that turned him into the implacable enemy of society who robbed and killed and then betrayed his accomplices without compunction. In his memoirs, published with great success by no less an editor than Dostoevski, he explained how his life was but 'a long drawn-out suicide; I belonged no longer to myself but to cold steel . . . society will have my blood but I, in my turn, will have the blood of society'. As a metaphysician, Lacenaire longed to find a meaning in life. Finding none, he sought revenge on society for denying him a simple truth. In 1835, with two companions, he was arrested for a robbery in which a widow and her son had been killed for a meagre 500 francs. The poet was sentenced to the guillotine. Disdaining a death outside Paris ('not for anything in the world would I have consented to deal with a provincial headsman'), he met his end in the capital. Lacenaire was strapped into the *bascule* (the platform that holds the body rigidly in position) and the machinery swung him beneath the blade. The executioner pulled his lever, the razor-sharp edge flashed downwards – only to jam mere centimetres above his neck. The blade was hauled up again, the mechanism checked, the lever pulled. Once more the hurtling knife stopped a fraction above its victim's head. As the whole process was started once more

Lacenaire managed to twist his head and stare upwards at the plunging blade. It plummeted downwards a third time, as the poet watched it come. This time it did not jam.

Lampart Don Guillem de *(burnt to death 1659)*

Despite his name, de Lampart was an Irish adventurer (his original name was William Lamport) who pretended that he had been appointed Viceroy of Mexico. He was eventually arrested and remained in prison, on and off, for seventeen years before the authorities decided to burn him at the stake in 1659. Being a man of determined character and independent mind, he pulled his bedclothes over his head whenever the priests tried to talk to him and even at the stake itself he succeeded in defeating his persecutors' intentions, hurling himself against the iron fixture by which he was attached to the stake and thereby dashing his brains out, so that only his lifeless corpse was consumed by the flames.

Languille *(guillotined 1905)*

The head of this guillotined criminal was subjected to an interesting experiment by Dr Beaurieux at the very moment it tumbled forward from the blade on 28 June 1905. The good doctor observed movement in the eyelids and lips and three times called out Languille's name in a loud voice. The first two times he did this, the eyes opened and focused upon him; on the third attempt there was no reaction.

Lovat Lord *(beheaded eighteenth century)*

This eighteenth-century Scottish rebel was beheaded by the public executioner, but for some obscure reason his family arranged for his head to be sewn back on again. The famous *aficionado* of public executions George Selwyn attended on this occasion not only the decapitating but also the recapitating, where he evoked gales of merry laughter among those present by giving a comical imitation of the Lord Chancellor's voice saying: 'My Lord Lovat, your lordship may now rise.'

Maccabees family *(tortured to death first century BC)*

According to this description by the Rev. Henry Southwell in his *New Book of Martyrs*, these were the methods by which the Syrian tyrant Antiochus Epiphanes attempted to convert a Jewish family of a mother and seven sons away from their own monotheism and back to idolatry.

Maccabeus, the eldest, was accordingly stripped, stretched on the rack and severely beaten. He was next fastened to a wheel and weights hung on his feet till his sinews cracked. Afterwards his tormentors threw him on to a fire till he was dreadfully scorched; then they drew him out, cut out his tongue, and put him into a frying pan, with a slow fire under it, until he died . . . After the second son had his hands fastened with chains, with which he was hung up, his skin was flayed off from the crown of his head to his knees. He was then cast to a leopard, but the beast refusing to touch him, he was suffered to languish until he expired with the excruciating pain and the loss of blood. Machir, the third son, was bound to a globe until his bones were all dislocated; his head and face were then flayed, his tongue cut out, and being cast into a pan he was fried to death. Judas, the fourth son, after having his tongue cut out, was beat with ropes and then racked upon a wheel. Achas, the fifth son, was pounded in a large brazen mortar. Areth, the sixth son, was fastened to a pillar with his head downwards, slowly roasted by a fire kindled at some distance, his tongue was then cut out and he was lastly fried in a pan. Jacob, the seventh and youngest son, had his arms cut off, his tongue plucked out, and was then fried to death. Salamona, the mother . . . was, by the tyrant's order, stripped naked, severely scourged, her breasts cut off, and her body fried until she expired.

Mallet Claude Françoise
(conducted his own firing squad 1812)

A general in the French revolutionary army, Mallet
converted his own execution into something like a scene
from a Marx Brothers' movie. Mallet had unsuccessfully
attempted to overthrow Napoleon by a cunningly planned
coup in Paris while Napoleon's invasion of Russia was
beginning to founder in 1812. Mallet's achievement in
almost bringing off his *coup* was considerable, since he
organised it while he himself was in prison. Condemned to
death, Mallet sought and was granted one privilege – that,
as an old general, he should be permitted to give the order
to the firing squad that was to shoot him and his
co-conspirators. When he gave the order for the squad to
aim, they did not move in proper unison, whereupon
Mallet gave them a stern dressing down and proceeded to
put them through a quarter of an hour's drill, giving the
final order to fire only when he suddenly realised that the
suspense had reduced his fellow-victims to a state of
complete nervous prostration.

Manichaeus *(flayed first century)*

This unorthodox early Christian philosopher was also a
practising faith healer. He was skinned alive and fed to the
dogs when he failed to cure the son of the Persian king.

Manlius Son of *(executed on his father's order)*

The unfortunate son of Manlius fell victim to one of the
cruellest pieces of paternal authoritarianism ever
recorded. Manlius was a Roman general who had gained
much fame by accepting a challenge to personal combat
with one of the enemy and by vanquishing the challenger.
Later he forbade his own troops to engage in combat
without permission, but his son, remembering his father's

famous victory, accepted a challenge from one of the enemy chiefs. Like his father before, he won the fight. When he laid his trophies at his father's feet, the latter had him executed for disobedience.

Maquer Chevalier
(strangled on the gibbet at Montfaucon 1400)

This execution followed Maquer's confessing to the murder of Aubry de Montdidier in the forest of Bondy, near Paris. Maquer had killed Montdidier in secret and had buried his body under a tree. However, Montdidier's faithful greyhound had been present during the murder and subsequently took one of Montdidier's friends back to the spot and uncovered the body. The dog then proceeded to attack Maquer whenever it saw him, causing him to come under suspicion. Then ensued, by command of King Louis VIII, the most remarkable of medieval trials by combat. On the island of Notre-Dame, Maquer was buried up to his waist in the ground and given a shield and stick with which to defend himself against Montdidier's greyhound. The dog was given an empty hutch in which to take rests. The dog soon got through Maquer's guard and took him by the throat; Maquer screamed out a confession of murder, and the dog was pulled off so that the murderer could die on a gibbet.

McCallum Frank *(suicide in gaol 1857)*

Otherwise known as Captain Melville, McCallum was an Australian convict turned bushranger who was said to have been the guiding spirit behind the stoning to death by prisoners of the infamous John Price in a quarry at Port Gellibrand in 1857. Price was a sadist who held the post of Inspector-General of Convicts in Victoria, and before that had been known as 'the monster of Norfolk Island' for the cruel and often fatal punishments that he inflicted there for breaches of discipline. McCallum certainly had a reputation for attacking warders and it came as no surprise when, in August 1857, he died in his cell at Melbourne Gaol. The verdict of the coroner's jury, however, was somewhat surprising. They determined that he had strangled himself with his own hands.

Mesfiwi *(walled up alive 1906)*

The Moroccan cobbler Mesfiwi, who murdered up to thirty women in Tangiers, was made to pay for his crimes in a particularly horrific manner, Originally it was suggested that the killer should be publicly crucified, but when this was deemed too barbaric, he was given an alternative fate: to be immured alive. As a screaming mob jeered his every plea, a team of masons steadily built up a wall around the doomed man. Even when the wall was completed and Mesfiwi vanished from sight, the mob refused to leave, revelling during the next two days at his gradually weakening screams and entreaties. When on the third day the noises had ceased, the mass murderer was pronounced dead.

Monmouth James, Duke of
(incompetently beheaded 1685)

After the failure of his rebellion against James II in the late seventeenth century, this natural son of Charles II was sentenced to death. It took the executioner no fewer than five successive blows to accomplish his task. After the execution, the body and head were returned, sewn back together and dressed up. A picture that was painted of this apparition is in the National Portrait Gallery in London.

Morton James Douglas *(guillotined 1581)*

Morton, as Regent of Scotland, had made a visit to Halifax to watch a novel method of execution – a sliding block with knife attached that fell straight down, between two poles, and severed the neck of the unfortunate who had been placed below. On his return north of the border, he had erected a similar proto-guillotine, known as 'the maiden', for use against criminals in Edinburgh. The name comes either from the Celtic *mod-dun* (place of justice) or, more likely, as a copy of the Italian *Mannaia,* a name for a similar machine which had been used in Italy since the thirteenth century. It may have given some posthumous pleasure to the shades of those Morton had had beheaded that, when he himself fell from grace in 1581, he suffered his fate at the blade of his own machine.

Oppenheim Joseph Suess *(strangled 1738)*

Financier and adviser to the Duke of Wurttemberg in eighteenth-century Germany, when the duke died Oppenheim was executed on charges of graft and profiteering. How much truth there was in the charges is difficult to assess; there was little documentary evidence against Oppenheim, but his enemies attributed this to his cunning rather than to his innocence. He was executed on 4 February 1738 by being placed inside a cylindrical iron cage, two and a half metres high and just over a metre wide, which had been made in 1596. He was then strangled and hung up like a dead bird inside the cage, strung from a gallows eleven metres high.

Osborne Mrs *(lynched 1751)*

On 30 July 1751 this poor woman was the last person to be lynched as a witch in England. (The last official execution for witchcraft in England was in 1682; in Scotland, 1722.)

Mrs Osborne was seized from the local church, where she had been barricaded in the vestry for protection, and given the water test – being dragged through a pond until she drowned. The individual who gave the lead in this barbarous act had the gall to go around among the spectators collecting money as payment for the entertainment he had provided.

Pariseau N. De *(beheaded by mistake 1793)*

Pariseau was director of the ballets at L'Opera in Paris at the time of the French Revolution. Although a strong supporter of the Revolution, he was arrested in 1793 and executed by guillotine in the mistaken belief that he was a captain of the king's guard named Parisot.

Parthenius *(castrated and strangled c.100 BC)*

Executed during the reign of the Roman Emperor Nerva about 100 AD for complicity in the killing of the previous emperor, Domitian, Parthenius had his genital organs torn off and thrust into his mouth, after which he was strangled.

Phalaris *(roasted to death 563 BC)*

Tyrant of Agrigentum in the sixth century BC, Phalaris made himself notorious by his cruelty, particularly by his use of a hollow bronze bull as a device of torture and execution. The victims were placed inside the bull, under which a roaring fire was got going; the screams of the roasting victims, reverberating within the bronze body and emanating from its mouth, sounded lie the roaring of a real bull. It was typical of Phalaris that the first person to be made to suffer death in this way was one Penicus, the artist who had constructed the bull in the first place. When he was finally overthrown in 563 BC, the citizens placed Phalaris himself inside the bull and dispatched him over a particularly slow fire.

Ravaillac *(tortured to death 1610)*

François Ravaillac murdered King Henry IV, 'Henry the Great', of France. The court was less than lenient in its sentence. After the lengthy torture of the *brodequin* – a box into which, after the foot was placed in it, a series of wedges were driven, gradually reducing the bones in the foot to pulp – Ravaillac was paraded in the streets of Paris through massive and extremely hostile crowds. At first the hand which had killed the King was placed over a fire. His body was pinched and torn with red-hot pincers, and once there were large enough wounds melted lead and scalding oil were applied to every one, intensifying the agony. After several hours of such torture, his limbs were affixed each to a horse and for thirty minutes, at intervals, these horses tried to dismember him. In the end, enraged that the horses had failed in their grisly task even after thirty more minutes' tugging, the mob rushed in and used swords, knives, sticks, any weapon that came to hand to hit, slash and mangle the wretched Ravaillac. Once they had torn him to pieces, they took various bits around the city and burned them on a number of bonfires.

Regulus Marcus Attilius *(rolled to death c.256 BC)*

Regulus, a Roman consul, was executed by the Carthaginians. The method employed was to seal the unfortunate Roman inside a barrel which was liberally studded inside with sharp nails and spikes. The barrel was then rolled down a bumpy hill. Those sealed up did not survive their journey down the hill.

Ridley and Latimer, Bishops *(1555)*

The story of the burning of Ridley and Latimer at the stake in 1555 is familiar to most of us. Less widely known is the fact that Ridley's brother thoughtfully supplied two little bags of gunpowder that he tied around the victim's necks, the intention being that in each case the fire would cause a mercifully quick and fatal explosion. This did not in fact happen. Latimer died quickly, asphyxiated in the smoke, before the flames had reached the gunpowder, while Ridley lingered for a long while, screaming, 'Let the flames come near me! I cannot burn!' Both men are commemorated in the Martyrs' Memorial in Oxford.

Ripoll Cayetano *(garrotted 1826)*

Ripoll was a poor schoolteacher whose fate it was to be the very last person executed as a heretic by the Spanish Inquisition. This took place as late as 1826 in Valencia. He was garrotted but, instead of being burned at the stake in accordance with previous custom, his body was enclosed in a barrel on which flames had been painted in scarlet and then buried in unconsecrated ground.

Rodriguez Anna *(burnt at the stake 1682)*

Rodriguez was the oldest victim of the Spanish Inquisition. She was burnt at the stake on 10 May 1682, aged ninety-seven.

Ross Norman *(gibbeted 1754)*

Ross was executed in 1754 in Edinburgh and left hanging from the gibbet, common practice at that time. The monster Nichol Brown, who was subsequently hanged for roasting his wife to death over the kitchen fire, tore off part of a leg from Ross's suspended remains and took it to a Leigh alehouse, where he grilled it over the fire and ate it for supper in front of a group of horrified acquaintances.

Rudge, Martin and Baker *(hanged 1886)*

In 1884 hangman James Berry was travelling on the Great
Northern Railway from Doncaster to Durham when he
found himself sharing a compartment with three
rough-looking men who started chaffing him, jokingly
claiming he must be the hangman on his way to the
forthcoming execution. Berry pretended not to
understand what they were getting at, but they persisted
and began to joke amongst themselves, offering bets as to
which of them Berry would get first. Two years later,
Berry met them again. Rudge, Martin and Baker were
condemned to death for murdering a policeman, and
Berry encountered them this time on the scaffold at
Carlisle in his official capacity.

Selurus *(eaten by wild beasts first century)*

In ancient Rome, Selurus was an outlaw who was
condemned by Augustus to be executed by being dropped
into a cage of wild animals. His death proved to be so
spectacular that it gave considerable impetus to the
fashion for executing criminals by throwing them to the
lions in the arena during the Roman Games. Tigers, bulls,
leopards, wolves, bears, dogs, elephants, even crocodiles
were also used as public executioners in this way. Oddly
enough, these animals needed to be intensively trained to
ensure they carried out their part in the show. Living
slaves were fed to them for weeks beforehand so that they
would get the taste for human flesh, but, to ensure that the
valued animals were not damaged by their victims, the
latter had their teeth removed and their arms broken first.

Smith Gill *(hanged 1738)*

Smith was an apothecary from Dartford. Living way
beyond his means, with a pack of hounds and more like a
country squire than a simple tradesman, he had fallen into
debt. He insured his wife for £200 and attempted to
recoup his losses by murdering her and gaining the
money. The murder came off, most brutally, but Smith
was arrested, tried, convicted and sentenced to hang.
Throughout his last days he conducted himself with
remarkable sang-froid. Chained to the floor in the gaol, he
demanded supper and hoped they weren't going to forget
his hunger. When he was searched he declared that he had
no knife and would rather kill off the whole world than
harm himself. He ate and drank whatever was available,
usually cracking jokes to those who brought it. Told that
he was due to be hanged in chains, he merely called for
more food, saying, 'If I am to be crow's meat, I'll live
accordingly.' It so happened that one Hardy, well known
for his prowess on the French horn, was visiting the prison.

Smith asked him, as a personal favour, to attend the
hanging and play some hunting calls as he was taken to the
scaffold. Once the date of his execution was announced he
remarked only, 'Well, if that be so, there'll be a room to let.'
On the way to the gallows he smiled and waved happily to
the crowds, enjoying nosegays that he had managed to
procure. Finally, as the noose was adjusted, he gave the
crowds a broad smile.

Sowrey Alfred *(hanged 1887)*

Here is James Berry's account of the hanging of Alfred
Sowrey at Lancaster gaol in 1887 for shooting his fiancée.

He was half-dead with fear by the day of the execution . . . he
became seriously ill through sheer terror, and it was thought that
he could not possibly live to the day appointed for his execution.
The efforts of the jail chaplain to bring Sowrey to a calmer and
more reasonable state of mind seemed utterly unavailing; the
prisoner was too terrified to take much notice of anything that
was said to him . . . from the cell to the scaffold, he had to be
partly pushed and partly carried by two warders. in whose arms
he struggled violently. His groans and cries could be heard all
over the prison. His teeth chattered, and his face was alternately
livid and deathly white. Every inch of ground over which the
procession passed was violently contested by the criminal, who
had to be bodily carried up the steps and placed on the drop. As
he saw the beam above him, a wilder paroxysm of fear seemed to
seize the miserable youth, and four warders were required to
hold him in position. Even with this assistance I had the greatest
possible difficulty in pinioning his legs, and while doing so I
received a nasty kick which took a piece of bone out of my shin,
and has left a mark visible even today. After the completion of
the pinioning process he still resisted the placing of the noose,
throwing his head violently from side to side, and he continued
his struggles until the drop fell. During the whole of this terrible
scene the chaplain . . . continued reading the beautiful prayers
for the dying; but Sowrey paid no heed.

Sprecage Antonio *(prolonged hanging 1919)*

Sprecage was hanged for murder in Canada in 1919. Due to an incompetent hangman his death, rather than taking the supposedly 'painless' few seconds, actually dragged on somewhat longer. It was one hour and eleven minutes before the prison doctor could pronounce the killer properly dead.

Strangeways Major George *(crushed to death 1658)*

Major Strangeways was a Royalist who had no desire for his estate to be sequestered by the Roundheads and thus leased it to his sister, Mabellah, with whom he lived. When Mabellah became engaged to be married, the major, appalled at the thought of his estate being lost to a husband of whom he disapproved, murdered the man. To plead guilty would have meant forfeiting the estate to the Protectorate, and Major Strangeways refused to do so. At this refusal the court ordered the process known as the *peine forte et dure* – in other words, pressing to death. The sentence commanded:

that the prisoner be put into a mean room where no light can enter, that he be laid upon his back with his body bare, save for something to cover his privy parts, that his arms be stretched forth with a cord, one to each side of his person, and in like manner his legs shall be used, that upon his body shall be laid as much iron and stone as he can bear and more, that the first day he shall have three morsels of barley bread, and the next day he shall drink thrice of water in the next channel to the prison door, but no fountain or spring water, and this shall be his punishment till he dies.

Friends requested that he should be placed on boards with a projecting piece – thus snapping his spine and speeding his death, but the gaoler refused. Instead these friends, who were able to attend the torture, quickly jumped on the already painfully weighted board and thus ended his sufferings.

Tarpeia *(crushed to death)*

The daughter of the governor of one of the Roman citadels was crushed to death beneath the shields of an invading host of Sabine warriors, to whom she had traitorously thrown open a gate. The Tarpeian rock, from which traitors were thrown to their death, was named after her.

Vickers Robert F.
(executed by hanging while unconscious)

Vickers was convinced he would be reprieved, and right up to the last moment was continually asking whether the reprieve had arrived. Even on the scaffold he showed every sign of genuinely expecting a reprieve at any minute. At the precise moment when the noose touched his neck, he fainted clean away, and the trapdoor was then released.

White Charles *(hanged 1827)*

Charles White, a bookseller of Holborn, was condemned to die after he was found to have burnt down his shop in an attempt to defraud his insurance company. For a city that could still shudder over tales of the Great Fire of London a century and a half previously, arson ranked second only to murder in the catalogue of punishable crime. White lost all trace of self-possession in prison, on the ritual ride to Tyburn and on the scaffold itself. He very adamantly did not want to die. Tearing free of his bonds, he stood in the cart, raving, weeping, screaming and begging for mercy. On the drop he managed to tear the mask from his eyes. As the drop fell he lunged desperately at the platform, only to be kicked into space by the hangman. He then gained a purchase on the rope and attempted to haul himself up it, trying to preserve what remained of his life. As the crowd watched his hideously contorted features, he fought his losing battle with fate, his tongue protruding, his whole face a mask of pain and fear. Finally, as the hangman dragged on his flailing legs from below, he gave up his grip, and with it his life. It was this nauseating public spectacle that led eventually to the prohibition of public executions, and their continuation behind prison walls.

Witzleben General Erwin Von *(executed 1944)*

With others involved in the unsuccessful attempt to kill Adolf Hitler with a bomb on 20 July 1944, Witzleben was strangled on 8 August by being hanged by the neck with piano wire suspended from a butcher's hook in Plotzensee prison. The event was recorded on sound-movie film for showing that same evening to Hitler, who had personally decided upon this method of execution.

Myth and magic

Anonymous German
(victim of prophecy ninteenth century)

A native of Berlin met a fortune teller and was only too
quick in telling the seer that he, for one, had nothing but
contempt for his so-called skills. To which the fortune
teller, out of nothing but a sense of pique, told him that
without a doubt he was destined to end his days on the
scaffold. At first the Berliner pooh-poohed such prophecy
but gradually he began to question his scepticism. Perhaps
the man was able to tell fortunes, in which case . . . Soon he
became obsessed by his awful fate. At first he considered
suicide, but realised that, by committing a mortal sin, he
would forfeit any chance of a pleasant afterlife. He then
decided, to ensure gaining the approval of the Almighty,
to have his life cut off by Justice in the form of the courts.
In other words, he must become a murderer. Religion
once again prompted his actions. Reasoning that, were he
to kill an adult, this might involve sending a soul to Hell, he
decided to kill a child on the principle that such a
youngster could not have committed a sin and, dying in
innocence, would naturally speed straight to Heaven.
With this theology duly satisfied, he did kill a child, the son
of the man for whom he worked, and in due course
fulfilled most painfully the fate he had been promised.

Anonymous Hungarian hypnotist *(knifed 1936)*

A popular, but now anonymous, Hungarian hypnotist was
giving his standard performance in the small town of Izsak
one evening in 1936. As usual he called for a volunteer to
help with the show. A young farmer, Karoly Szani, duly
offered himself and was soon deep in a trance. The
hypnotist began to give him directions: 'Here is a knife.
Take it. Stand up. Here comes one of your enemies. You
hate him because he has stolen away your sweetheart.' The
farmer responded to order, and his mentor pursued the
subject. 'Look out! Your foe is about to attack you! Get
him!' Szani sprang forward and stabbed viciously with the
knife, thrusting it fatally into the hypnotist's heart. The
performer was rushed, in vain, to hospital. Poor Szani was
dragged back to reality by a local doctor. He remembered
nothing of his involuntary murder.

Anonymous Scottish man
(imagined himself to death nineteenth century)

Sir Walter Scott was told by a medical friend about a man
who was killed by the power of his imagination. First, he
imagined he saw a large cat that repeatedly appeared
before him in circumstances that clearly indicated it was
hallucination. Next, the cat stopped appearing and he
started to have recurring visions of an elaborately dressed
gentleman. After a few months, this phantom appeared
no more, and instead he started seeing a skeleton. He then
wasted away and died.

Anonymous Venezuelan fisherman
(buried alive 1974)

A nameless Venezuelan fisherman appeared to be dead.
He was duly placed in his coffin. It was of little help to him
that he woke from his trance – only to find himself sealed

up. So horrified was he by his premature burial that the shock gave him a heart attack. No new coffin was required.

Baglin Carol Anne *(religious rite victim 1973)*

In February 1973 Carol Anne Baglin, a part-time model and former star school athlete, was one of a five-member religious cult who lived communally in Hampton, Victoria, Australia. The household included Carol Anne, David Phipps, 27, Antoinette 'Toni' White, 24, James Cendrillon, 21, and Alfons Klimek, 17. The tenets of their religion eschewed drugs, materialism and 'lusting', and they were obsessively tidy and clean in their home. Dustbin lids were polished with boot polish, window frames scrubbed with pot scourers, dirt scraped from cracks in concrete. Phipps and Toni White lived as a couple, as did Carol Anne and Cendrillon, but it was deemed that their relationship was evil and that they must give up all sexual intercourse. When Carol Anne claimed she found such abstinence difficult, the others joined together in night-long 'encounter' sessions in which, under a barrage of criticism and questioning, they would attempt to 'purify' her with constant questions about 'lusting' and her thoughts on sex. These sessions often went beyond the merely verbal and became violent, both physically and in the lengthy screaming and abuse. Victims, who had included Neomi Klimek, Alfons Klimek's sister, told how they would crack and admit anything, no matter how perverse, to answer their accusers. The group was obsessed with sex, depravity, drugs and what they claimed, in these endless rantings, were their concomitant evils. Carol Anne was marked down as a deviate, but she was as obsessed as the rest. She saw sexual symbolism everywhere, in bananas, rubber hoses, even the vacuum cleaner. Such admissions merely exacerbated the attacks and she made a terrible error in admitting that physical pain, to whit beating and slapping, with belts, hands or whatever, brought her to a climax. At one session she also claimed doubtless under duress, an attraction to Phipps. For the last two and a half weeks of her life, Carol Anne Baglin endured daily beatings that lasted from thirty minutes to two hours every time. On Sunday 24 February she was undergoing her regular workout when she mentioned the phallic vacuum cleaner. Toni White 'pushed her and she fell over'. As she fell Carol Anne's head smashed into a sharp, hard object. Thinking she was pretending, the others dumped her into a cold bath. But she was not pretending. She had died, as the government pathologist revealed, of a subdural haemorrhage when her head smacked the cleaner. At the trial White and Phipps, who now revealed himself as one Robert Jacobson, were gaoled for three years, while Klimek and Cendrillon, also guilty, were put on probation for four years. Carol Anne's father, a 43-year-old boiler attendant, placed his daughter's ashes on his mantelpiece, a vase of red roses on either side.

Barley Florence *(drowned 1931)*

Maid-servant Florence Barley, twenty-three, worked at a large house near the Buckinghamshire village of Chalfont. In the way of such villages, there was an unhappy romantic legend concerning the local pond. Once, it was told, a young girl had waited at the pond for a lover who never arrived. Wretched and distraught, she had thrown herself beneath the waters and there drowned. Ever since, it was claimed, anyone so foolish as to run three times around the pool would see the dead girl's hand protruding above the water. When someone told young Florence the tale, she replied contemptuously, 'What a silly girl.' On 12 September 1931 Florence visited her father and gave him some money, telling him, 'Give this to Mum.' Then she left. The next morning she was reported missing. The search lasted five days before someone thought to check the fatal pond. A group of villagers gathered to stare at a patch of dank weeds out in the middle. There, thrusting above the water, was a girl's hand, beneath it lay a corpse: the remains of Florence Barley.

Bathurst Benjamin *(vanished 1809)*

The precise manner of Bathurst's death is and will almost certainly remain unknown; but his extraordinary disappearance on 25 November 1809 represents one of the classic mysteries of all time. He had been in Vienna on official British government business during the Napoleonic Wars and was returning to England through Germany when he stopped briefly at the White Swan Inn in Perleberg. After dinner he called for his horse and carriage, stood outside in the presence of several other people, watching his luggage being loaded into the carriage, stepped round to the heads of the horses and from that instant was never seen again.

'Brown' Lieutenant *(victim of a magician c.1916)*

Brown was a pseudonym given by Dr J. Johnston Abraham in his memoirs to a soldier who died a mysterious and sinister death in Egypt during the First World War. Abraham was the medical officer in Brown's unit, and was responsible for caring for Brown when the latter returned sick from leave in Cairo. It transpired that Brown had allowed a local magician to touch his eyes with a silver probe, on the pretext that this would give him the power to see with his eyes closed. On the way back to his unit, he had come down with a fever. The next day he was delirious and babbled that he could in fact see through closed eyelids; then suddenly he died. At the post-mortem Abraham found a tiny black spot, the size of a pinhead, in the inner corner of the white of each of Brown's eyes. Three hours later the black spot was as big as a pea. After another three hours it had covered the inner half of each eye. After yet a further three hours the whites of both eyes were completely black. No other bodily abnormality was found. The eyes had not been punctured and the cause of Brown's death remains a mystery.

Browne John *(communicant of the supernatural 1654)*

A well-attested manifestation of the supernatural occurred as Browne lay dying in 1654 in Durley, Ireland. At the end of his bed sat a large iron chest with three locks, containing family papers. As his relatives stood by his bedside, they saw the chest slowly open of its own accord,

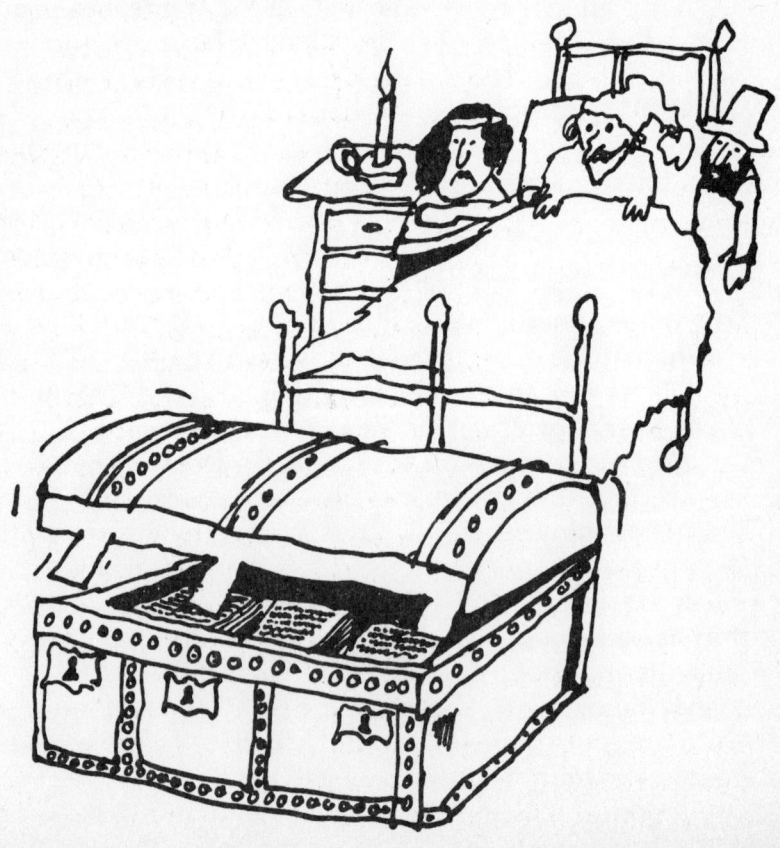

each lock in turn being released and the lid rising to an upright position. Browne, who until then had been virtually comatose, opened his eyes, sat up in bed and spoke these words to the open chest: 'You say true, you say true, you are in the right. I'll be with you by and by.' He then lay down again in bed and, as the chest slowly closed and the locks re-engaged, he died.

Carnarvon Lord, *et al.*
(killed by a curse 1923 and onwards)

'Death will come on swift wings to those that disturb the sleep of the Pharoahs' – so runs the curse that threatened those who in 1923 launched a successful expedition to open the 3,000-year-old tomb of Egypt's boy-king, Tutankhamun. Not only that, but four different fortune tellers warned the expedition's leader, Lord Carnarvon, against carrying out his plans to enter the tomb. Despite all these considerations, Carnarvon entered the tomb in February 1923 and set about extracting its treasures. Two months later he awoke one morning in his hotel room to announce, 'I feel like hell.' He did not survive the day. He fell into a coma and, the same night, he died. Death was attributed to a mosquito bite, but the superstitious noted that the bite was in exactly the same place as a blemish on Tutankhamun's body. At the very moment of death, it was also pointed out, every light in Cairo was momentarily extinguished. The trail of deaths associated with Tutankhamun's tomb is impressive and frightening. Just a few days after Carnarvon, an American archaeologist, Arthur Mace, told his companions, 'I feel terribly tired.' He fell into the same coma and died before doctors could diagnose his illness.

The deaths multiplied. The Hon. Aubrey Herbert, Carnarvon's half brother and witness to the opening of the tomb, remarked, 'Something dreadful is going to happen to our family.' He died on 27 September 1923. George

Gould, a close friend of Carnarvon's, rushed to Egypt on hearing of the problems. Twenty-four hours after his visit to the tomb he was dead. The radiologist who x-rayed the mummy, Carnarvon's secretary and his father, a British industrialist who was an early visitor to the tomb, all died in mysterious, unaccountable ways. By 1930 only two of the original expedition were still alive.

One of the survivors, Richard Adamson, has twice attempted to 'challenge' the curse on television. On both occasions his appearances were followed by near-miraculous escapes from sudden death, as well as the death of his wife and serious injury to his son. When in 1972 the Tutankhamun exhibition came to London, the original organiser died within hours of signing the papers for the sending of various relics to London. His successor, Dr Gamal Mehrez of Cairo Museum, remained a sceptic. He decried any fears, saying, 'I don't believe in the curse for one moment.' The day Tutankhamun's golden mask was sent off to London, Dr Mehrez dropped dead. The cause was allegedly circulatory collapse. Of the six RAF crewmen who flew the exhibition to London, three suffered accidents or losses and two died. Since then the deaths seem to have abated – but then so has interference with the remains of King Tut.

Ceynowa Anna *(murdered as a witch 1905)*

Anna Ceynowa was unpopular amongst her fellow-residents of Putzig, a village on the Baltic coast of Poland; so much so that seventeen of them declared her a witch and set out to rid their community of her presence. Such spiritual cleansing was easily accomplished. The godly band abducted Anna from her cottage, blindfolded her and flung her into the icy Baltic from a rocky promontory, named Hela. Despite the blindfold she managed to swim ashore, but even this proved futile: as she mananged to drag herself from the waters, her persecutors surrounded her and strangled her to death with the lengthy tresses of her own hair. The murderers then blithely presented themselves at the police station, just as a matter of record, to announce that they had performed a vital community service. It was to their great surprise that they were arrested and jointly charged with the murder of one they still declared a 'sorceress'.

Constantinova Anna *(drowned 1933)*

According to a centuries-old legend, the so-called 'Vampire Lake' near Varna in Bulgaria demands each year a human sacrifice on the same fateful day. Not unnaturally, on the appointed day only the foolhardy among local peasants dare approach the lake, let alone bathe in it. One such, however, was Anna Constantinova who, in 1933, either forgot the tradition or deliberately chose to flout it. Whatever the cause, the effect remained the same. No sooner had young Anna stripped off and plunged in for her bathe than the Vampire Lake lived up to its terrible name and she found herself sucked beneath the waters and drowned without a chance of rescue.

Council Catherine *(murdered in exorcism 1977)*

Twenty-one-year-old Catherine Council of New York City died when her mother became convinced she was possessed of the Devil. Mrs Council consulted a 'root doctor' who provided her with a potion, based on a mixture of ammonia and turpentine, to drive Satan out from young Catherine. Mrs Council took her daughter out in their car, before tying her up, placing a towel around her face and force-feeding her the exorcist's potion. Catherine Council died under these ministrations; the cause of death was listed as asphyxiation secondary to suffocation.

Cruz Manuel and Viana Miguel
(killed by a UFO? 1966)

The unmarked bodies of these two UFO investigators
were found on top of a hill near Rio de Janeiro in 1966.
They had gone up the hill wearing raincoats and leaden
face-masks shortly before a glowing shape was seen to
hover overhead. The cause of death was never established.

El Cid Rodrigo Diaz de Bivar *(1099)*

El Cid, the Spanish leader in the war against the Moors,
commanded that, were he to die in battle, his corpse
should be embalmed and then seated on his horse,
Babieca, during the next battle. El Cid was wounded and
did die, and his instructions were carried out. At the next
battle, an attack on Valencia by King Bucar of Morocco,
when the Spanish seemed on the verge of defeat, the
preserved body of their leader, mounted on his horse,
appeared at the head of the troops. The weary Spanish
rallied at this sight and drove the Moors in confusion from
the field.

Emery Professor Walter
(victim of a curse twentieth century)

A British Egyptologist died of a stroke at the very moment
when he had just discovered and was handling a statue of
Osiris, the ancient Egyptian god of death (*see* Carnarvon, *et
al.*).

Erceldoune Thomas of *(vanished 1297)*

Sometimes called Thomas the Rhymer because of his
poem about Tristram and Yseult, and known far and wide
as a soothsayer, Erceldoune's death, or at least his
departure from the land of mortal man, occurred in a

rather beautiful way. One day, as he was entertaining the Earl of March in his home, a hart and a hind, normally the shyest of forest creatures, appeared on the outskirts of the village and quietly made their way through the astonished villagers to Thomas's dwelling. He immediately rose from his table, recognising that he was being summoned, and followed the two animals back into the forest, never to be seen again.

Freeman Edith *(sacrificed to God nineteenth century)*

A five-year-old girl was sacrificed to God by her father in late-nineteenth-century England. He declared that God had instructed him to kill Edith and had promised that she would rise again in three days. He improvised an altar out of a table in his house, laid the little girl upon it and stabbed her to death with a knife. After this he barricaded himself in the house to await his daughter's resurrection on the third day. When arrested, he announced that he was a second Abraham. His act was universally reviled, and all agreed that he had been driven insane by attending too many revivalist meetings.

Greenhaulgh Letitia *(killed in exorcism 1907)*

Resident in the ironically named Zion City, New York, the unfortunate Mrs Greenhaulgh fell foul of her son, daughter and several other citizens who had taken it upon themselves to drive out the devils they were convinced had taken up residence in the old lady's frail body. Her two children plus three others were members of the Parhamite sect whose fundamentalist precepts gave them *carte blanche* to inflict a terrifying series of tortures on the old lady. The five fanatics knelt first at her bedside to pray before starting to jerk and twist her limbs. As she cried out in pain, the workout merely intensified as the triumphant quintet struggled harder to silence 'the devil's tongue'. When, at

length, Mrs Greenhaulgh's neck was broken by the
beating, the 'demonic' shouts did indeed cease. It was only
when the Parhamites started stage two, the resurrection of
the old lady, that their faith met less malleable facts. All
five were arrested and tried for the murder of Mrs
Greenhaulgh.

Hatton Bonose Duke of Franconia, Abbot of Fulden and Archbishop of Mayence
(eaten by rats)

Archbishop Hatton began his prelacy with great mildness
but when, in the second year of his rule, a drought
overtook his archiepiscopy – the country around the River
Rhine in Germany – he revealed traits that were more
barbaric than benevolent. So tormented was he by the
endless beggars turning up at his palace demanding bread
and aid that he had them all collected in a barn – perhaps
500 in all – promising a distribution of food to the needy.
In the event, when the people had collected, Hatton had
the barn sealed, then set fire to the place, massacring in the
flames everyone there – men, women and children. To
compound his crime, he announced that in his view such
beggars were no more than vermin and deserved to be
treated as such. Soon after this, it was reported, a vast
number of rats gathered at the palace and started
attacking the archbishop. He was unable to fend them off
and he tried to avoid their bites by throwing himself into
the Rhine. He then took refuge in a tower that stood on an
island in the river, but the rodents swam the river and
pursued him in his last refuge. Overwhelmed by their
gnawing, Hatton died. Legend had the rats moving on to
eat up even notices in churches upon which his name had
been written.

Hug-Helmuth Dr *(murdered 1925)*

Freudian psychoanalyst Dr Hug-Helmuth treated, among other patients in her Vienna consulting rooms, her nephew Rudolph. Nineteen-year-old Rudolph was an orphan, placed in the care of his aunt after his parents had died. He had money but little ambition and soon turned into a wastrel and general ne'er-do-well. His aunt watched his development with dismay, and worry gradually turned to real fear as she became convinced that Rudolph intended her death. Only weeks before the doctor's body was found strangled she had written to a colleague: 'My whole life is now an expectation of a blow. I am terribly uneasy. I see myself with him standing before me and then squeezing me round the throat.' With horrible accuracy Dr Hug-Helmuth had predicted all too well. One night in March 1907 Rudolph did enter her room in the middle of the night and did choke out his aunt's life as she slept. In his defence the young man claimed that he resented his aunt's use of him as a guinea-pig for her analytical theories and that he especially loathed a book she had written, based on his own condition, to extol the value of psychoanalysis. This had little effect on judge or jury, and Rudolph Hug was sentenced to twelve years in gaol for this murder.

Lang David *(vanished 1880)*

Lang was a farmer in Gallatin, Tennessee. In September 1880, Judge August Peck and a friend were driving to visit Lang on his farm. As their buggy pulled up the lane towards Lang, who was crossing a field, the judge was about to call out when Lang quite simply vanished before his eyes. Assuming that he must have tripped and fallen into a crack in the earth, the two men, plus Lang's wife, who had seen the vanishing act from the house, rushed up to see what had happened. But there was no crack, nor any other logical reason for the farmer's abrupt and mysterious exit. Lang was never seen again, although a year later it was said that faint cries for help were heard near the spot. To underline the mystery, no farm animal would ever go near that part of the field again.

Lyttleton Lord Thomas *(died of a dream 1779)*

This young nobleman had various talents but lived a dissipated life. One night in 1779, at the age of thirty-five, he dreamed that a woman dressed in white appeared before him and gave him a solemn warning that he would die in three days. Three days later, Lord Lyttleton arranged for a party of his friends to spend the night with him, and when the appointed hour came he jokingly observed that it looked at though he had beaten the ghost. Reaching out for a fresh drink with which to celebrate, he experienced a sudden sensation of faintness and was assisted to bed, where he died.

Michel Anneliese *(exorcised to death 1976)*

This young West German girl died of starvation in 1976 as a result of a mental disturbance that her parents and a number of well-meaning local clergy were convinced was really a case of possession by the Devil. Anneliese's mother remembered that when she was pregnant with Anneliese, a mysterious old hag had predicted that her child would be seized by the Devil. Her local pastor, a Jesuit priest, a bishop and another pastor sought to solve the problem by exorcism rites and procedures over a period of nine months. A total of eighty-six hours of exorcism sessions were conducted, without success. Anneliese continued to have convulsions and to blaspheme in strange voices, one of which was Adolf Hitler's. Finally she stopped eating and died. Her parents and two of the exorcists were convicted of homicide by negligence.

Miller Glenn *(missing 1944)*

Bandleader Glenn Miller, fresh from entertaining troops in Britain, was preparing to move on to Paris. 15 December 1944 was a cold, foggy day and Miller, among others, was less than keen on the idea of flying the Channel. An eyewitness who saw him climb into the plane heard the worried query, 'Hey, where are the parachutes?' He also heard the reply from Miller's gung-ho pilot, USAF Major Norman Baesell. Echoing the First World War Marine sergeant's exhortation to hesitant troops, he quipped, 'What's the matter, Miller, d'you want to live for ever?' With that the plane lumbered into the air. It never arrived in Paris. Neither wreckage nor bodies were found to satisfy researchers into the precise cause of the bandleader's disappearance, but suffice to say, he has yet to feature at one of the many 'Glenn Miller Revival Nights'.

Mudd Norman
(drowned and strangled twentieth century)

A young disciple of the self-styled 'Beast' and ostentatious diabolist and drug addict Aleister Crowley, Mudd used to introduce himself to people by saying, 'My name is Mudd'. Somehow Mudd incurred the hostility of his master Crowley, who laid a curse on him, condemning him to death 'by water and the rope'. Mudd was found dead on a beach in Portugal, drowned and with a rope around his neck.

Newcombe Phyllis *(spontaneous combustion 1938)*

Phyllis Newcombe, twenty-two, was dancing one evening in 1938 at Chelmsford Shire Hall in Essex. As she spun round the floor in the arms of her fiancé, she suddenly and uncontrollably burst into flames. No efforts could quench the fire and Miss Newcombe died of her burns. No explanation for this bizarre outbreak has ever been satisfactorily put forward.

Newell Patrick *(drowned 1971)*

A young high-school student of Vineland, New Jersey, drowned in 1971 in bizarre circumstances. He was obsessed with the study of Satanism and the practice of occult rites, and used to hold secret ceremonies at which hamsters were offered to the Devil as blood sacrifices. He had a group of friends with whom he performed these practices, and one day he announced to them that in order for him to become a leader of demons it was necessary for them to tie his hands and feet and throw him into a local pond. This they did.

Nixon Mrs *(preserved 1926)*

When Mr H. Hughes, an auctioneer of Crewe, acting under an order in bankruptcy, entered a house in Nantwich, he found it occupied by three sisters named Nixon. After breaking down the barricades the sisters had erected, he was met by the trio with their hands uplifted. One intoned, 'We are in God's hands. This is God's house. There is fire and brimstone in every room. Mother must not be touched. She is in God's hands.' Her soul may well have been so ascended, but the corporeal remains of Mrs Nixon were far from with her Maker. Close to a couch in the kitchen the appalled Hughes discovered a skeleton wrapped in a sheet. In front of the skeleton was a table on which stood fruit, nuts, bread, butter and a bowl of tea. Another sister instructed the auctioneer, 'That is God's table. Don't touch it.' A third sister told him they had not been to bed for five years but ever since their mother's death had kept a vigil with the decaying body in the kitchen. The sisters were subsequently removed to an asylum; it is not recorded whether Mrs Nixon was finally given a more traditional resting place.

Parfitt Owen *(disappeared eighteenth century)*

This eighteenth-century pirate simply disappeared, like a
conjuror's assistant in a stage illusion. Having suffered a
stroke that had left him incapacitated, he lived in
retirement in a country cottage under the care of a female
relative. One day she left him sitting in his wheelchair
outside the cottage, enjoying the sun, while she went to a
nearby shop. When she returned, having been away only
briefly, his chair was empty and there was no sign of him.
Some workers, who were within sight and earshot of the
cottage and who would have spotted anyone arriving or
leaving, had seen nothing. Still in the chair were the
cushions and rug with which Parfitt had been made
comfortable.

Pierce Ruth *(died for lying 1753)*

In 1753 a group of women were arguing in the market
square of Devizes, Wiltshire, over their respective
contributions to a joint purchase of wheat. Ruth Pierce
kept some of her contribution hidden in her hand but
swore that she had already paid in full, declaring that she
was ready to be struck down dead if she had not. After
repeating this statement, she fell down and died on the
spot.

Price Jesus Christ *(early cremation 1884)*

This curiously named child died at the age of five months
in 1884. The significance of his death lies in the fact that
the attempted cremation of his body by his father, Dr
William Price, gave rise to a test case in the courts that led
ultimately to the legalisation of cremation. Dr Price was a
druid and a vegetarian who became the father of Jesus
Christ at the age of eighty-three. (His housekeeper was the
mother and she subsequently had two other children by

the sprightly octogenarian, one of whom was named Jesus Christ the Second.) On Sunday 13 January 1884, the villagers of Llantrisant found Dr Price, dressed in his white druidical robes, trying to burn Jesus Christ's body with petrol at the top of a hill. This caused a near riot, and Dr Price was obliged to take the half-burned body back home, where he kept it under the bed for a week. He was brought to trial but found not guilty of any offence.

Rehmeyer Nelson *(burnt to death 1928)*

Nelson Rehmeyer, a Pennsylvanian farmer, was wont to dabble, with a number of companions, in the 'magic art' of voodoo, more usually expected in climes more exotic than bucolic North America. It was when he allegedly 'bewitched' the family of an eighteen-year-old boy who also practised the black arts that Farmer Rehmeyer found himself in trouble. A friend of the bewitched boy, eighteen-year-old William Hess, went off to a local 'witch doctor' who said that the spell could be removed by taking a lock of Rehmeyer's hair and burying it eight feet beneath the ground. For this advice he charged a forty-dollar fee. The two boys and the 'doctor' immediately visited Rehmeyer to demand the requisite curl. Not surprisingly the farmer was reluctant to make himself party to this exorcism. This was an error; enraged by his refusal, the 'doctor' and his youthful accomplices then set upon Rehmeyer, knocking him cold with a chunk of wood. Then they removed the desired lock of hair, soaked the unconscious farmer with kerosene and set fire to his clothes. He died in the fire.

Rich Lady Diana *(died of smallpox seventeenth century)*

Lady Diana Rich was daughter of the Earl of Holland and a noted seventeenth-century beauty. The fate of Lady Diana has been quoted as evidence for the traditional belief that to meet one's own *doppelganger*, or double, is to know that one's death is imminent. She was walking in her father's garden at Kensington, according to John Aubrey, to get some fresh air before dinner, when she was suddenly confronted with her own precise mirror image walking towards her. At the time she was in perfectly good health; but she died of smallpox within a few weeks.

Saiyi *(died of 'sympathetic' bullet wound 1919)*

Saiyi was an Indian civil servant and tiger man – someone who believed that his soul was magically linked with that of a particular tiger. In March 1919, on hearing that a local tiger had been shot and wounded, Saiyi declared this tiger was his own *alter ego* and took to his bed. He experienced severe pains in the abdomen and had to be taken to hospital where inflamed swellings were found on either side of his body, corresponding to the entrance and exit holes of the bullet that had struck the tiger. Before long he died, apparently of the peritonitis that a bullet would have caused.

Schoenberg Arnold *(died as he predicted 1951)*

The composer Arnold Schoenberg had a lifelong obsession with numerology. Born in 1874 on 13 September, he was convinced that 13, traditionally an unlucky number, would play a vital part in his death. The numbers 7 and 6 make 13, thus he believed that his seventy-sixth year would be the decisive one. On consulting the almanac for that year, 1951, he saw that 13 July fell on a Friday. When the fateful day arrived, he stayed in bed, hoping to reduce all possibility of an accident. Just before midnight his wife came up to see him and reassure him that all his fears had been foolish. The composer turned towards her, murmured his last word, 'harmony', and died. The time was 11:47 p.m. (which

numbers add up to 13), thirteen minutes before midnight
on Friday 13 July, in his seventy-sixth year.

Schraetus Ulrick
(carried off by Satan seventeenth century)

This death evidently comes from the world of legend
rather than historical fact, yet it is recounted by
Theophilus Lucas, in his *Memoirs of the Gamesters* (1714),
with enough detail to indicate there must have been some
original basis for the story. Schraetus was playing dice with
two other men on a Sunday, near Bellizona in Switzerland.
Having lost almost all his money, he staked what remained
on a final throw, swearing that if he lost this time he would
plunge his dagger into the very body of God, as far as he
could. He lost. Drawing his dagger, he hurled it into the
sky, where to the astonishment of all present it
disappeared, and several drops of blood fell on to the
table. Immediately Satan appeared and carried Schraetus
away with a terrible noise and stench. The other two
gamblers; half crazed with fear, tried unsucessfully to rub
out the blood from the table; but before long one was
struck dead, 'with such a number of lice crawling out of
him, as was wonderful and loathsome to behold'. The
other was quickly put to death by the appalled citizens of
the town.

Shambunath *(buried alive 1934)*

125-year-old Shambunath had been abbott of the temple
at Bhaironji in India for more than fifty years. Following
the tradition of centuries of predecessors the venerable
monk had himself buried alive, declaring to his fellows
that his useful life could now be considered over.

Slown *(died of fright)*

A man died, apparently of fright, in an underground passage at Netley Abbey in Hampshire. The passage was said to contain a terrible secret. Slown's last words were a screamed 'Block it up! In the name of God!'

Stewart John *(killed seventeenth century)*

Otherwise know as the Juggler, Stewart was a wandering charlatan in seventeenth-century Scotland who was rash enough to claim possession of magical skills. Inevitably he was arrested and charged with witchcraft. To prevent his committing suicide and thus avoiding official torture and execution, he was securely fettered in his cell in such a way that he could not possibly use his hands or arms. Yet a mere minute or so after two ministers of religion had left his cell, he was found dead, hanged by a length of rope from his cell door. It was immediately decided that he had been killed by his master Satan to prevent his revealing any infernal secrets.

Verdung Michael
(Burned at the stake fourteenth century)

Verdung was executed in medieval France as the result of an extremely unlucky coincidence. A traveller in Poligny, a village near the Swiss border, was attacked at night by a wolf, but managed to drive it off, injuring it with his sword. He chased the wolf and came across Verdung's cottage at the very moment that Verdung was having some sword cuts bandaged by his wife. It was at once assumed that Verdung was a werewolf, and he was punished accordingly.

Warren Leonard *(died of a heart attack 1960)*

Warren was an American opera singer. He was
performing in Verdi's *La Forza del Destino* at New York
Metropolitan Opera in 1960. The opera turned out to be
all too aptly named. He had just begun the aria 'O fatal urn
of my destiny'. When the singer reached the word 'fatal', in
full view of a fashionable audience, he suffered a heart
attack and pitched forward, dead.

Whittington Dr *(gored by a bull fifteenth century)*

A fifteenth-century bishop's chancellor was killed by a bull
in Chipping Sodbury, apparently in divine retribution for
his condemnation of an innocent woman to death at the
stake. As Whittington was in the act of supervising the
woman's execution, a bull escaped from the slaughterer's
axe elsewhere in the town and ran straight to the place of
execution, weaving its way through crowds of people
without attempting to harm any of them until it reached
Dr Whittington, whom it immediately charged and gored
to death.

Wood Ian *(cursed to death twentieth century)*

Killed by a curse? This young man from Sydney, Australia,
who dabbled in witchcraft and the occult, was preoccupied
with the death of his mother. She had died accidentally in
England when she walked over the edge of a cliff in a fog.
Since her death, Wood had believed that he had been
cursed by a witch and that as a result he would not live to
the age of twenty-seven. He died at twenty-two. His body
was found at the foot of a small cliff in rocky bushland.

Bibliography

A number of books, magazines, newspapers and other media sources, even occasionally word-of-mouth, were investigated for the purposes of compiling these deaths. Obviously one cannot list every one, and sometimes research has noted the facts but forgotten the source, but here for those who might like to read further in this area or who, perhaps, doubt the veracity of some of the more bizarre specimens of demise, are the main sources.

Anger, K., *Hollywood Babylon*, 1975
Anon., *Augustan History*, n.d.
Brewer, E. C., *Dictionary of Phrase and Fable*, rev. ed. 1981
Bryson, W., 'Bizarre Ways to Bow Out', *Mayfair*, June 1978
Fiedler, L., *Freaks*, 1978
Gibbon, E., *Decline and Fall of the Roman Empire*, ed. Low, 1960
Glaister, *Medical Jurisprudence and Toxicology*, 1910
Gould, G. M. and Pyle, W. L., *Anomalies and Curiosities in Medicine*, 1896
Green, J., *Directory of Infamy*, 1980
——, and Atyeo, D., *Don't Quote Me*, 1981
Harvey, Sir P., *Oxford Companion to English Literature*, 3rd ed. 1946
Haydn, *Dictionary of Dates*, 1904 ed.
Hibbert, C., *Roots of Evil: Social History of Crime and Punishment*, n.d.
Ives, G., *Man Bites Man*, ed. Sieveking, P., 1980
Maunder, *Biographical Treasury*, n.d.
Nash, J. R., *Bloodletters and Badmen*, 1973
Anon., *The Newgate Calendar*, 1932 ed.
Nowra, L., *The Cheated*, 1980
Sitwell, E., *English Eccentrics*, 1933
Smith, Sir W., *Classical Dictionary*, 1898
Suetonius, *The Twelve Caesars*, trans. R. Graves, 1957
Swain, J., *A History of Torture*, 1931
Tacitus, *Annals of Imperial Rome*, n.d.
Anon., *The Terrific Register*, vols 1 and 2, 1825
Wallace, *et al.*, *The Book of Lists*, vols 1 and 2, 1977, 1980
——, *The People's Almanac*, vols 1 and 2, 1975 1978
Wilson, C. and Pitman, P., *The Encyclopedia of Murder*, 1961
Winslow, F., *The Anatomy of Suicide*, 1840

Index